GOODBYE DOCTOR

Drs Leslie Poidevin and Walter Pye, June 1986

Goodbye Doctor

STORIES OF COUNTRY PRACTICE

Leslie Poidevin

Published by the Author

JULY 1986

ISBN 0 9588361 0 8

Wholly photoset, printed and bound by
Gillingham Printers Pty Ltd
Adelaide, South Australia

Contents

Introduction

I was thirty-one years old when, at last, I was permitted to get on with my life in the medical profession. Having recovered from almost four years of Japanese overlordship, and the excitement of my return to freedom, I was most anxious to get back to my practice in Scone with Walter Pye. Because he had carried on alone through the war years, he too was anxious for our partnership to return to normal. He had many plans for its expansion.

The reader will detect several themes in these pages.

The underlying delight and happiness is evident in my return to a beautiful country district and a partner whom I regarded with great affection and admiration. The reminiscences, which are mostly humorous, cover many different situations which were experienced by country practitioners. They will show the community respect given to the doctor. In the 1940s this respect was mutual, highly regarded and treasured by the doctors.

The beginnings of the breakdown in the doctor/community relationship will be detected, as will the replacement of the dedicated and compassionate doctor by his commercial successor.

Not only is the mystique of the word 'Doctor' disappearing but also the person himself who 'wore' it. The more it is usurped by other sections of society the less significant it becomes.

It will not be difficult to detect the beginning of a successful marriage, nor the happy way of life experienced by the country doctor and his wife.

These stories, recalled from memories alone, are all based on factual experiences. Because many characters have been forgotten, others have been invented for the sake of the story. The timing of many events and even the places and names have been manipulated to avoid any disrespect, offence, disloyalty or hurt to anyone. Should these efforts of mine have failed, I apologise.

Our patients came not only from Scone but from many other towns and villages. Looking back on my life there, forty years ago, I have no doubt that medicine, as practised then, was far more agreeable than is possible today. We were lucky.

The era of these stories has gone . . . so . . . 'GOODBYE DOCTOR'

L. O. S. Poidevin MD, MS, FRCOG
BURNSIDE SA 1986

With a Touch of History

There was trouble at 'Invermein' early one morning in May 1940. Harold Cowdrey had summoned me to meet an invasion of some gastro-intestinal wog which was disturbing the peace there.

One hundred years earlier there had been another invasion at 'Invermein'. Police Commander Nunn made a cavalry charge across the paddocks of 'Invermein', which were then being grazed by the Littles and the Halls. Earlier he had collected some thirty troopers at Jerry's Plains in response to the 'kill the blacks', campaign.

The lead-up to this campaign began three or four years earlier. Reports had told of tribes of Aborigines massing in many areas of New South Wales and Victoria where the squatters had brought their cattle and sheep. The Aborigines objected to this and were mounting a campaign to repel the invaders, who, since the crossing of the 'Blue Mountains' in 1815 had moved so far and fast in search of new grazing lands. The passing of the 'Border Police Act' of 1839 had encouraged the Aborigines to attack the squatters. They became more aggressive, and renewed their attacks on squatters and their stock. So successful were they that all squatters were driven off the Liverpool Plains, where no grazing took place from 1840 onwards for several years.

These activities of the Aborigines could well be considered the world's first expression of 'black power'. It was in response to this that the police invaded the paddocks of 'Invermein' and 'Puen Buen' in 1840.

So much for 1840. It was now 1940. There was trouble again and much activity at 'Invermein'. The rapid movements now were all directed towards the bathrooms.

'Invermein' homestead must have been one of the earliest colonial types in the Scone district. When I first saw it in May 1940, it was set a long way back from the road and surrounded with wide verandahs. All the doors and windows were handcrafted in cedar, dowels rather than nails, dated their construction. The rooms were large, leading off an entrance hall, in which I remember seeing an old fashioned music box, for the first time. A large central courtyard, with a stone floor, one step below the level of the house, had to be crossed to reach the enormous kitchen and the servants' quarters. Beyond this was a block of cells, then used as stables, in which the convicts had slept. As evidence of this there were large steel rings anchored to the walls with a number, in Roman numerals, below each ring. My memory of the details is hazy now, though I was most impressed on my first visit.

My return to the surgery led me into the usual situation of far too little time to do far too much.

It was not until after dark that my thoughts returned to 'Invermein'. What had happened? I had heard nothing all day. Were they all dead? Or had they recovered?

Back at the household I found things had improved. The only disaster occurred when the old and confused cook, seeking to attend yet another call from nature, rushed into the wrong room and sat on the kerosene heater!

Peace came to me at last as I sat in the old leather chair sipping the whisky Harold poured me while I listened to him, telling me of the radio news which had dominated the day. I learnt of the massive evacuations taking place, on the other side of the world . . . at Dunkirk. What a day!

Sleep did not come easily. I agonised about the war news while I debated my future. I lost. I decided to join the AIF.

CHAPTER ONE

Beginning Again

'Thank goodness that's over,' I thought to myself as I put my car back in the garage at 2.30 am on the 1 January 1946, at 'Waawaarawaa'. The last two hours had been spent at 'Brancaster' the maternity hospital in Park Street, Scone. I had been called to the confinement of Mrs Dalton, having her fifth child at about midnight on New Year's eve. No one expected any difficulty as Mrs Dalton was always 'very quick'. Events shortly after midnight proved this to be quite true, the product of her fifth birth lay screaming and contorting on the end of the bed. The kidney dish was waiting, with the severed cord, for the delivery of the after-birth. This was where the trouble began and my confidence quivered. The placenta did not come. Mrs Dalton, whose experience far exceeded mine in these matters, said, 'You push hard on my tummy and I'll give a good shove'. Only blood filled the kidney dish. 'Try again', she said. More blood!

It was then that Sister Batterham touched me on the shoulder and suggested we just wait a little while.

As she walked me to the kitchen she said, 'Doctor, the best way to handle a reluctant placenta is to go and have a cup of tea'.

I remembered her saying this to me in 1940 on a similar occasion when we sat in that large kitchen with the wood stove and the large sooty kettle, always at 'the boil', ready for emergencies such as this.

So much had happened since then. Much as I hated doing it, I had volunteered for the AIF when Italy came into the war. After such a little time in partnership with Walter Pye following my resident days at Royal Prince Alfred Hospital, I felt I had to leave him and do my bit. He was married and had been in practice in Scone since 1932, so I was the obvious one to go.

After much preliminary fooling about in army camps in New South Wales I eventually was posted to 'Sparrow Force' for the defence of Timor. In February 1942, we were overwhelmed by a massive Japanese force eventually surrendering when we were surrounded with dead and wounded. I became a prisoner of the Japanese and spent nearly four years as their guest in many prison camps.

As a doctor I was more fortunate than most, for there was always an abundance of medical work, and, particularly for me, surgical work in Java. This was an all male society.

Here I was, terrified, to be back among women patients having babies. I had thought little about these things for more than four years so I was really dangerous. I needed 'Batt'.

The tea was strong, and the thinly cut bread and butter plentiful, as I sat and looked at that wise old face. 'Batt', who was then seventy years of age and had helped several generations of women and their doctors, had a waxy skin on her flat face, but her eyes had the mischievous sparkle of one who knew the answers.

As I hurried through my large cup of tea and appeared anxious to go back and see Mrs Dalton, she put her hand on mine and said, 'Have faith doctor, Mrs Dalton won't let us down'.

My faith was not that strong as my thoughts flashed back to the Royal Hospital for Women in my student days, when I watched, with excitement, Dr Bruce Williams demonstrate a manual removal of a placenta. Would I be equal to the challenge of such a massive intrusion into the womb to separate this placenta? My war service had proved to me that I had medical courage but cowardice gripped me now.

What a way to begin the New Year!

After the second cup of tea, when 'Batt' decreed, I was allowed to return to Mrs Dalton who had been left alone for twenty minutes. Had she haemorrhaged into unconsciousness, would I have to face a manual removal?

'It's all right doctor', she said as I walked in, 'I've pushed it out'.

There was the after-birth in the dish, quite complete. As I put my hand on her tummy to feel the firm contracting uterus, I once again thanked my gods.

So many times in the past few years I had felt this inner excitement at 'having been let off again!' The fears of those prisoner of war years were different from this recent fear. In the prison camps I not only experienced the fears of my medical inadequacies, but there was always the overriding fear, to all of us, of the wretched Japanese, with all their inhumanity.

When I got back to bed I could not sleep. My thoughts kept going back to Brancaster. It was a large old cottage converted long ago into a hospital for midwifery, in Park Street, run by Sister Batterham. Her life had been devoted to her work and now she owned this hospital. It was set back about twenty feet from the front gate which led up to the front door across a wide verandah. The central hall was wide with brown linoleum as its cover. The labour ward, where one's quick steps were usually directed, was the second door on the right. The large kitchen was two doors further down also on the right; beyond was a large central bricked courtyard off which were several bedrooms. A wing with

2

eight more rooms had been added shortly before I arrived. So there were about twelve bedrooms as well as a nursery for the babies.

In today's language such an institution would be unacceptable and condemned by government health authorities, but in 1940, when I first went there, and until 1951, when I left, Brancaster was the venue for many hundreds of successful and happy births. There was no operating theatre there so our difficult problems were transported by ambulance, up the hill, to the Scott Memorial Hospital where there were excellent operating facilities. This had been named in remembrance of Scone's first long-serving and respected general practitioner.

After a fitful sleep I awoke, at daylight, to a New Year's Day of 102 degrees fahrenheit, feeling lonely and afraid. Walter Pye, my partner, who had carried on our practice without help since I left in 1941, till these last few days of 1945, had gone off with his wife for a most deserved rest from the heavy responsibilities of this busy country practice.

Walter must have been crazy to leave this responsibility to me—so I thought, for I was afraid and alone—but he probably thought it was the best way to handle me. Such a lot of rot was being talked about how to handle returning prisoners of war of the Japanese—the psychiatrists, whom neither of us regarded with any authority on this question, were preaching 'kid glove' therapies, whereas Walter showed me the deep end. His parting remarks, as he left for his holiday, were—'Do your best and remember patients are awfully hard to kill!'

Miss Richards was left in charge of the house and to care for me. When Walter bought 'Waawaarawaa' and the practice in 1932, she had come to him to run the place until his marriage in 1935. Her brother was the manager of one of Scone's banks so she stayed on there, always in readiness to fill the breaches as they occurred. Here she was back in charge again in 1946.

The New Year's Day only required a visit to the Scott Memorial Hospital for rounds and a call at Brancaster.

A rodeo was the town's main excitement for the holiday, to which I was taken by Vic Hall, an old friend of Walter's, whom I think had been deputed to 'keep an eye on me'.

I was reintroduced to the sport of bulldogging and rough riding, challenges which were readily accepted by the young bloods who came in from the outlying stations. Beer was plentiful, so as the afternoon wore on, the horse and cattle games reached fever pitch. It was not greatly exciting to me and I only hoped there would be no broken necks.

Several of my old patients, from my pre-war year in Scone, came up to talk to me, showing some interest, supposedly to see if I had gone 'nutty'. I was glad when Sergeant Bedingfield rescued me by asking me to attend a motor car accident on the main road near Parkville, five miles north. Vic came with me to find a Chevrolet car had gone off the road and overturned when the driver had probably gone to sleep—it was a straight stretch of road, often the scene of these accidents. No one was seriously hurt so the only entry in the day book remained the confinement of Mrs Dalton. This four guineas entered on 1 January 1946 was the first fee I earned in my new life in Scone.

My real week's work began next day after Miss Richards had made sure Beatrice, the housemaid, had three dishes on the hot plate on the sideboard; sausages, fried eggs and bacon. With toast and coffee, these were ready each morning at eight.

My hospital rounds at the District Hospital, more intensive than the day before, brought surprised faces and disappointed remarks from patients of their beloved Walter Pye. Mrs Higgins, who had had her gall bladder out twelve days earlier, was excited when I allowed her up out of bed to sit on the verandah. Jimmy Ralph had fiddled around with the extension ropes on the fracture bed so his fractured thigh needed readjustment on the Thomas splint. Mrs Pauling, whom Sister had warned me about, bored me with her anxieties about her bowels, while all the other patients required my introduction and of course, my sympathy. I realised I was on trial, but I was enjoying it.

The morning ritual of tea in the Matron's office was special this day as Mr Poole, the secretary, and the three senior sisters, heavily starched, were all invited to meet me on my return from the war. The Matron and sisters were new since my year there in 1940, though Mr Poole knew me well. Dr Toby Barton, the other doctor of our Scone trilogy, wandered in to join us. He was then about mid fifty, whose war stories hinged round his days at Gallipoli and the Dodecanese Islands. He was a gentle fellow who had been a general practitioner in Scone since the early twenties, and related his stories with a twinkle in his eye. His practice was not large but was made up of old faithfuls.

After my visit to Brancaster to see Mrs Dalton and her baby and three or four other new mothers, I prepared for my first morning's consults, shaking at the knees.

The waiting room was not empty, which I had feared, knowing Walter's popularity, so I called in the first patient. After listening to her story and after the examination, I suddenly realised what was to be my greatest problem for the day. I would have to write prescriptions. The five years since I had done this found me wanting. I fumbled about looking for help in the drawers of the desk without relief, so I excused myself and went up into the house where I sat and tried to remember what one ordered for a bladder infection. In our prisoner of war camps there were never any drugs to be ordered, but a little way along Kelly Street I knew Mr Barnett had a chemist shop full. Was it hyoscyamus and potassium citrate for cystitis? Didn't one add some tincture of belladonna? I found a small pharmacopoeia and eventually scribbled what looked like an intelligent prescription, all drugs written in Latin

4

with Roman numerals and quantities. The instructions, again in Latin, ordered the usual eight ounce bottle made up with chloroform water and some infusion buchu to give it the expected nasty taste.

That hurdle over I called for the next patient. It seemed that little Johnny Adams had worms. His mother had seen them and Johnny was always eating but losing weight — lucky worms. What should I do now? Something strong and nasty was needed. Was it Thymol, or did I remember there was such a thing as Gregory's worm powder? In my dilemma I did what I found, usually, to be a helpful lurk. I asked the mother what she had already tried, thinking I would get a lead. Not so, this didn't work. She had been forcing Castor oil down poor Johnny every second night. The worms enjoyed the oil but Johnny needed my help.

Up with my pen and full of confidence I ordered some thymol and epsom salts, reasoning that the thymol would stun the worms and the salts would carry them off, whilst in this stupid state. Another impressive looking script and so to the next patient, something more in my line to restore my equilibrium. Mrs Bonnette brought in her three children, Jane, seven; Mary, six; and Tom, five years of age. Mother thought the tonsils were the trouble. They were good children, each one allowed me to look over their tongues to see enormous infected tonsils and to experience the breath that went with them. These would all be removed on the next Wednesday, which day had been reserved for tonsillectomies for many years, at the Scott Memorial Hospital.

The last patient for the morning looked sick, was sweating and coughing badly. Pneumonia was not difficult to diagnose even though I was out of practice with the stethoscope. I was full of confidence now as I arranged his admission to the hospital, knowing that I would have time to check up on his treatment before I went up to write his notes.

Just as I was leaving the surgery to go into the house the phone rang. Mr Barnett, the chemist, wondered if he might talk to me.

'Of course, what about?'

'What have you got against Johnny Adams? The usual dose of thymol for worms is about 30 grains, given in a powder form. If I read your writing properly it seems you have ordered 30 grams, which I think is a bit much. In fact I would say it would be dangerous'. 'Oh goodness me, how careless of me. Thank you for bringing this to my notice. Will you correct the dosage?'

'Yes, of course doctor. But there is another thing. You have written the prescription ordering it to be mixed with Epsom salts. This is most unusual. Do you mind if I make a suggestion?'

'No, do tell me what I should have done!'

'Well, I think I should make up some thymol powders in a cachet, say about 10 grains in each, and get him to take one in a sandwich with every meal and then the next morning take the Epsom salts'.

'Would that be safe, do you think?' I asked meekly.

'Oh yes, quite safe, but whether it will cure him of worms or just make him feel lousy I am not sure. But if you like I shall tell his mother to try this for a week and then to take him to see you again. Would you agree?'

'Yes, that would be fine, thank you Mr Barnett. While you are there, tell me, are you speaking from the shop?'

'No doctor. When I find it necessary to speak to the doctors about their prescriptions I always go back and use my house phone. It's much safer that way.'

'Well, thank you again Mr Barnett. You do realise I have got out of practice at writing prescriptions in the last few years. I shall call in and see you and get hold of some help. You know Walter Pye is away which makes it a bit awkward for me.'

What was it Walter had said to me—'Patients are hard to kill'. Not for me!!

CHAPTER 2

My Jumbuck Problem

That first day's work on 2 January 1946 was a real trial for me, on my own, in that highly respected general practice in the Upper Hunter. I felt the responsibility. I began to wonder whether I would ever reach the stage in medical practice where I would not feel the 'weight of the world' on my shoulders. My thoughts, as I lay in bed after the day's work, awaiting sleep, returned naturally to those most responsible situations and decisions I had to make as an army doctor, thrown into a wide range of surgical responsibilities, for which I was not only inadequately trained, but which scared me more than my Japanese overlords. * * * Those years were stressful and here I was feeling much the same. I hoped I could manage what came to me before Walter's return. Surely he would not leave me alone for too long! He had long since learnt to take the responsibilities of a respected country GP. I would have to, also, if I were to survive and become respected. 'What would tomorrow bring?', was my last waking thought.

The day was hot again and I wished I could have worn short pants and a cool shirt, but neither my conservatism nor the people of Scone were yet ready for such an indiscretion by their doctor.

I envied Alec Henderson, a grazier of some twenty miles out of town, when he came to the surgery towards the end of the afternoon's consult. He was a tall thin fellow with a large dark moustache, wearing light drill short pants, stockman's boots and a well worn wide brimmed hat.

'Would you have a look at a sick ram?' was his request.

I had seen him at the rodeo on New Year's Day and remembered him from my year in Scone in 1940.

'Are you joking? I know nothing about rams.'
'No I'm not joking, nor am I being disrespectful', he laughed.

'I've heard that you solved many awkward and odd problems during the war years, and as we've no vet available at present, I thought you might be able to help.'

Well, what's the matter with him?'
'I think his water works are gummed up. I noticed him lying down in the serving paddock, where he was supposed to be working. I thought he looked sick so I put him in the ute and brought him up to the shed.

* * * 'Samurais and Circumcisions' Gillinghams 1985.

'I've watched him for 24 hours now and I'm sure he hasn't pissed.'

'It's been pretty hot Alec, wouldn't that explain it?'

'I don't think so. I'm pretty sure about what I've told you and when he's touched on his belly he seems to be in pain.'

'Well, let's have a look at him'.

The ram was a much bigger animal than I expected. In fact I could never remember being as near as that to a ram before, so I really had no expectations. He was lying on some bags in the back of the ute. He gave me a pitiful look as I jumped up into the utility. I rubbed his head, thinking I should make friends with him and see how he behaved when confronted by a doctor in a white coat. He showed no response to this rather special consultation, until I palpated his lower abdomen when he made a rather odd 'ram noise' and tried to move away from my hand. He seemed to be in pain and I thought he was unduly swollen. It interested me to see the male equipment of a prize ram.

I began to realise why he had not passed any water for 24 hours. He had a full bladder and was obviously unable to empty it. What caused this problem, and whether it was common or not, I did not know.

Alec told me he had not had this problem before with any of his rams, so I gathered it was not common. He had been 'in sheep' for most of his life.

So there was the problem. A prize ram, worth a few hundred pounds or more, with a full bladder. I had passed catheters in men on many occasions, an art we had learnt as medical students, but I had never handled the male organ of a ram before. In fact it took me quite a time to learn where it was and to learn its capabilities.

'Do you think he will let me have a go at him Alec?'

'Oh sure, give it a go. I'll hold him down if he gives any trouble'.

So, having sterilised several catheters of various sizes, I took off my coat and mounted the utility for yet another 'first'. I had always regarded sheep as the stupidist of creatures, for many obvious reasons, as one watched them being handled, so I very much doubted my chances of success.

Having made myself familiar with the ram's penis, I selected what I thought was a suitable sized catheter and endeavoured to pass it along the urethra. It wouldn't go in very far, so I held the organ towards various points of the compass and twisted and pushed the catheter in various ways, only to be disappointed. Perhaps I should try another smaller catheter. Again I approached the penis with confidence while Alec leant firmly on the animal which, by now, was beginning to object to my attempts to help it. The smaller catheter seemed to go in further but I thought I could feel some obstruction very near the bladder entrance. I would try a stiffer type of gum elastic catheter. With more indignant objections from the ram, and greater efforts by Alec to restrain him my patience was being tested. As I felt what I thought was this area

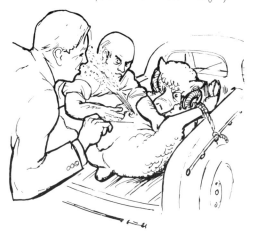

of obstruction, I became more confident and gave the stiff catheter a firm push, in what I thought was the right direction, to enter the hallowed sanctuary of the bladder.

Immediately urine came forth with such pressure that my search for success was rewarded with a thorough eye wash.

Great was the relief to all three.

Alec was delighted; the ram seemed to accept my efforts with obvious relief, while I wiped my face. I collected what I could in the kidney dish but it filled this more than twice.

After all this, Alec made sure his ram was restrained properly in the ute and came in for a whisky, well deserved by us both.

I discussed the question of veterinary services in Scone and learnt that visits from Newcastle were not infrequent, but were mainly to the many horse studs in the district. Farmers rarely used their services, it would not be economic. They did most services themselves. However, Alec was grateful for my help and suggested I forward an account but I felt the experience I gained was equal to the goodwill.

He took his ram home, while I wondered if I had heard the last of the problem.

Alec lived in the old Henderson house, a large country home with wide verandahs, set in the usual home paddock surroundings. The house was old and tired and the one thing I most remember about it was the monstrous bath in which he kept his polo sticks. He had played polo most of his life, and was an excellent horseman. Rightly or wrongly, I was impressed with the bathroom!

Within 48 hours Alec rang me with the same story. The ram could not pass its urine. What could I do about it now?

This call was not unexpected. I had been thinking about that obstruction which my catheter had to overcome to get into the ram's bladder. Did rams get a prostate problem, as old men got with advancing years? This was a question I had asked Vic Hall only yesterday. He denied ever hearing of it in rams. What about Charlie Kater, who had lived most of his life with all those fine sheep in Dubbo? Would he know? No, he couldn't help me. None of these chaps seemed to have any helpful textbooks either.

So, flushed with confidence, after my successful attempt with the catheter, and after much follow-up thinking about the ram, I suggested an operation. I explained to Alec that I thought there was some sort of tumour round the bladder neck, which was causing the trouble. I had no idea what sort of tumour it was and even less idea of what sort of operation to do, but if he wanted to take the risk and let me have a go, I was prepared to try. I asked about insurance of these prize rams but no, he had never insured any of his stock. He explained that any stock, sick or not performing, was usually shot. I therefore had a pretty free hand.

'Where will we do the operation?' he asked. I had thought about this and decided on the mortuary at the hospital.

'Couldn't we do it out on my property?' No, I had no inclination to set up operating conditions there. I would use the mortuary, thinking this was the rightful place for operation failures to end up.

That evening, after dinner, Alec arrived at the hospital with one of his men from the place as an extra helper. I had prepared my affairs but I wondered about an anaesthetic. Earlier I had learnt to anaesthetise cats by giving them a pentothal injection into a vein on the fore paw. Did sheep have easy veins like cats? I was pretty sure I could find a vein—if the ram agreed.

I cut off some wool from its front leg and shaved the skin where I found a suitable vein. The amount of pentothal needed would obviously be much more than in a cat, so I would have to make a guess. I explained all this to Alec, whom I put in charge of the anaesthetic department. Jim, his man, could help me open into the ram's bladder.

Alec was a good anaesthetist. We tied each of the ram's four legs to those of the table with ropes and Alec kept it asleep and breathing with an occasional push of the pentothal syringe.

I had opened the bladder, through the lower abdomen, on two occasions in the past, on soldiers, but this was easier. The bladder was full of urine and distended like a balloon. We let all the urine out and there, deep down, was a large cauliflower sort of growth. I guessed it was a fungating type of cancer, which didn't bode well for a cure, but if I removed most of it, the ram would probably be able to pass its urine. I found it easy to remove almost all of this tumour for it had a single pedicle which I tied without difficulty and cut it off. We kept the tumour which I intended to have examined at the Newcastle Hospital Pathology

Department. I closed the bladder wall using two layers of sutures and then the abdominal wall as I uttered the usual prayer of hope!

Alec took the ram and Jim home after Matron, who had shown much interest in our operation, had given us a cup of tea.

The ram recovered and took its place among the flock. Only time would tell whether it would be a useful member, and only the pathology report would indicate its prognosis.

I was rewarded with two bottles of whisky from Alec, and much personal satisfaction. News of the ram's operation and its recovery quickly spread. The doctor was 'good' with animals!

Scone was shortly to have an extremely fine veterinary service with highly qualified vets. This meant the end of my 'animal practice', and these exciting forays into unknown territory. Scone would be much better served now.

Strangely enough, Alec's ram lived a good life subsequently. The tumour was not cancerous and it suffered no post-operative complications. As far as I remember it lived out its life with its friends, probably boring them with the story of its operation.

I did enjoy country practice.

CHAPTER 3

A Pot-Pourri of General Practice

The den in 'Waawaarawaa' was the central room for me. The leather chairs and couch were well worn and gazed upon an 'Esse' slow combustion heater, a joy in winter. 'Monty' the Irish wolf hound spent most of his days occupying the whole couch. The walls were decorated with a full series of fighter planes of World War 1 vintage together with Walter's own Tiger Moth, hung over his desk. Only three years before my arrival there in 1940, his first partner and friend—'Blue' Houston, had crashed it on landing at 'Nandowra' when returning from a visit to Sydney. Vic Hall, on whose property this Scone airstrip was then located, was there to welcome his arrival which ended in a sudden nose-dive, killing himself and seriously injuring his wife. Walter, who himself was on his way out to meet them was confronted with this tragedy. He never flew again.

A large cedar door led from the den on to six steps which went down to the consulting suite. This we always referred to as the 'trap'. Movement back and forwards was easy and frequent, especially at afternoon tea time. The large sitting rooms and dining room were fashionably furnished by Gwen, Walter's wife. The floors were of highly polished Cypress pine boards with loose Persian rugs. A beautiful old cedar staircase led up to the bedrooms. I was to live here until my marriage later in the year.

After the day's work, three or four times a week, I would ring the one who had recently agreed to my proposal of marriage—Rosemarie Poole—in Adelaide. We had met, fallen in love and became secretly engaged within three meetings. Her parents wished to make the announcement in mid March — RM's 21st birthday. Thus I had to content myself with night calls by phone.

Telephone calls were always conducted through the telephone exchange so that Miss Trudgeon, the night duty telephonist was usually delighted when I asked her to call Rosemarie. Most nights were quiet on those manual exchanges; telephone calls were more for messages than for gossip, except for the doctor and his fiancé.

RM always had lots to tell me of her difficulties gathering a trousseau, whilst most items were still controlled and required ration coupons. She told of how her mother, a clever bridge player, made her many friends agree to play for ration tickets rather than the usual 3d per hundred. RM wanted to keep her job at the SA Housing Trust until March, to help her exchequer. Her search for the ring took up most of her lunch hours until it was found and then her wondering if I could afford it, all made interesting listening at the exchange. After twenty minutes or so of our conversation she would cut in and say—'Three minutes, are you extending doctor?' We would then carry on with bits about the practice and the preparations at my end. I was able to help with petrol tickets for we had far more than were needed.

These conversations, towards midnight, provided great listening for the exchange girls—what bliss, a forty minute call never cost more than the three minute rate.

The telephone exchange was in a building at the rear of the post office which occupied the corner of the main road through town—Kelly Street—and the main intersecting street—Liverpool Street—. This was the centre of Scone, with Campbell's large store on the opposite corner. The Golden Fleece Hotel and the Commercial Bank occupying the other two corners.

Scone's population then was about 2000 with an extensive district making a total of about 4000 for we three doctors to service. To the east, Barrington Tops, 70 miles away was our furthest boundary, beyond that one looked over the range to the coastal town of Gloucester. To the west we looked on Merriwa and Denman—30 miles—as our limit, with Murrurundi to the north and Muswellbrook to the south. So we frequently had a lot of driving to do when asked to visit outlying properties for their accidents or illnesses. The town was very similar to others of that size. Little had changed during the war years.

Scone was the centre of rich cattle, sheep and dairying industries in the most delightful fertile undulating country with distant hills. It was also the centre of the largest horse bloodstock breeding area of NSW with such well known studs as 'St Aubins', 'Kia-ora' (of 'Magpie' fame), 'Segenhoe' (of 'Talking' fame for which Alan Cooper paid £20000, a record sum then), 'Tinagroo', 'Puen Buen' and others. Many famous old established properties such as 'Belltrees', 'Ellerston', 'Waverley', 'Timor', 'Invermein' and many others graced the district.

Walter Pye, their beloved doctor, could never call at the post office box to collect the mail without being caught for one or more of his so-called 'kerbsides'. There were regulars who we thought used to wait, while others, in from their properties, usually had a medical question in amongst their greetings. Walter had spent three years in England in the late twenties studying for, and getting, his Fellowship of the Royal College of Surgeons and subsequently doing several house jobs in, what was then, a great service, the London County Council Hospitals.

He learnt to fly on 'Puss' Moths and to navigate by the railway lines.

On the ground his transport was a bull-nosed Morris Cowley which he bought for £10 when he arrived in England and left on the docks at Tilbury when he left. A gift for someone.

On his return to Australia in late 1931 his contemporaries begged him to join them in Macquarie Street but he harboured his own determination to establish himself as a first class country GP. He chose Scone, and bought the practice of Keith Grieve in 1932.

He was small, thin, with a determinaton most cleverly disguised and a charm which captivated whoever he was with. His ability as a doctor was well above the average which provided Scone with a specialist service that it had not had before. Dr Toby Barton, son of our first Prime Minister, was a much loved practitioner, held in high regard, but a product of an earlier age and without any specialisation. So Walter chose his town well and Scone benefited.

He quickly became the adviser to the Hospital Board which resulted in a new operating theatre and other modern facilities.

Fortune favoured me in late 1939, as I was deciding what to do about the war, when Mr McCulloch of Watson Victors asked me would I do a locum for Dr Pye in Scone for two weeks over Christmas and New Year. The twenty pounds a week and the chance to think for a while about the war made my decision . . . . . .

Well there I was without the 'prop', in 1946. After negotiating my first week, narrowly missing a few poisonings with the aid of my new ally, Mr Barnett, and being taught some of the tricks of feeding newborn babies and delighting in setting two fractures, an area of practice where my confidence had been gained at the war, I was reading the paper on Sunday morning when Vic Hall strolled in. He usually did this unannounced. He had never married, was then about fifty and, very lazily, running his ten thousand acres of run down sheep country. He was lonely and became a great friend.

As we were discussing his school days at 'Shore', where he had been an outstanding athlete, the telephone rang. The Anglican Minister, the Reverend Mr Turner, in the little town of Gundy, 15 miles to the east of Scone, was in great pain. 'Would you come out and see him doctor?', was the request from his wife.

My first country call since my return would be just the thing on this Sunday morning. The temperature had been over the hundred, most of the week, but now it was much cooler.

'Would you like to come Vic?'

Walter's practice car was a grey Morris 8/40 saloon, a very narrow little car with bucket seats.

The first half mile out of town was tarred, after that potholes and dust took over. Gundy was a little town on the Upper Hunter River with probably no more than 150 people. The Rectory was alongside the church and the parson was in considerable agony. Earlier in the morning he had got a sudden pain in his right loin which extended down to his right groin. A quarter of a grain of morphia combined with some atropine soon had him more at ease. He told me the pain came suddenly when he turned over in bed after waking up, as I was beginning to realise its cause. There was little doubt that he had a renal colic caused by a stone trying to get down from his kidney to his bladder. In the tropics, where we had sweated for the last four years, kidney stones were common and when they tried to get down the ureter to the bladder they caused jip. It was a well known saying – that 'little stones, like little dogs, make the most noise'.

As he settled down Vic was called in for tea and scones – always a ritual on country calls, when the medical problem could be discussed away from the patient.

I left Mrs Turner a syringe with more morphia and atropine ready for a further injection if needed during the night. There was an old nurse living nearby who could manage this.

The stone would probably pass down the tube to the bladder and then be easily passed in the urine. Mr Turner was asked to watch carefully for this. I would send out some medicine next day which should help.

As I was getting away there was a 'kerbside' waiting for me at the car. When the doctor was about, there was usually someone who just 'wanted to ask you a question about mother'.

Next day Mr Barnett our chemist got a bottle of medicine, containing potassium citrate and belladonna, on to the mail coach.

The only entry in the day book for that Sunday was four guineas for a normal confinement, which caught me just as I was going to bed. Ministers of religion were never charged for medical attention, so the visit and the 10/6 per mile usually charged, was gratis. This was quite happily accepted by most practitioners in those days, often the gratitude would come later in the form of poultry or eggs – and in this case the return of the syringe–plus the little stone.

My second week without Walter was much more organised, mainly because I had prepared prescriptions for most common problems, including ointments and creams and I kept these notes in the top drawer of my desk.

In the hospital I was taught about penicillin. We had a patient there who had pneumonia and the matron explained what a wonderful new drug this was. I had heard of it on my release in September 1945, but, of course, had not used it. It was said to be a life-saving drug but its method of administration was barbarous. Every three hours, 15000 units of the stuff had to be injected somewhere or other into a muscle. This was a considerable quantity of fluid which caused much pain. Our patient, who did not seem to me to be unduly ill, begged me to cease these frequent attacks, so I did just this, much to matron's horror.

My last four years' experiences with infections of all types taught me

15

pretty well when someone was really sick and we, of course, managed very well without penicillin. With this most solid experience I had no qualms about stopping these painful injections. Our patient was grateful and recovered without incident. That was my first introduction to penicillin.

There were many other more important things which I was to learn about, which had been developed while I was locked away.

The Rh (Rhesus) factor in the blood had been discovered, so important to women in their pregnancies. This discovery explained why so many women in the past had suffered with stillborn babies and why so many newly born babies died. It was learnt that the mating of an Rh positive male with an Rh negative woman could possibly result in disaster. This, I considered, was the greatest discovery I had missed out on.

Another one of particular interest to me, just being highlighted as I left for the war, was that discovered by Dr Norman Gregg (later Sir Norman) in his Macquarie Street consulting rooms, of the effect of Rubella (German measles) in early pregnancy on the developing foetus. I had some learning to do.

Another trap to watch for was the invasion of the drug companies into the pill making business. This would, in time, present far more problems and far more disability than my simple—usually ineffective—prescriptions, once I had learnt again the proper dosages. I preferred to see the traveller who measured me for my leather shoes than the one who extolled his company's new drug.

Somewhere about this time during an afternoon consult, there was an urgent knock on my door.

'Could I see you straightaway Doc?' a big distressed farmer asked.

'Yes, give me a minute until I just finish with this patient then I'll see you'.

'OK, thanks Doc'.

'Now, what's all this about?'

'Well, just look at this Doc' as the farmer pulled out his penis. 'Look at it, will it ever be any good again?'

He was pretty upset and I wasn't that happy. His penis was burnt and blisters were appearing on it. His pubic hairs had gone. 'How did this happen?' I had to know.

'Well I was pulling the harrows with my Massey tractor when the carburettor caught fire. I had no water with me so I pulled him out and peed on it. I'd had a few beers for lunch, so I had plenty of piss'.

'Did you put out the fire?'

'Yes, only just, but now look at me'.

'Now don't worry, I'm sure we'll get you fixed up OK'.

I sent him up to the hospital after wrapping up his 'problem' and rang the sister.

He settled down by next day when he saw our treatment would fix him, but the ward didn't. His story kept them amused for days. Me too. Farmers are a resourceful lot!

The most worrying case I had during those two weeks was a hefty young man who was a boundary rider on a large mountain property near Barrington Tops.

He had driven seventy miles into town because for three days he had pain in his testicles and his scrotum was becoming swollen. He spent his days in the saddle which gave me a clue to what I thought was the diagnosis, although I had never seen a case.

When I examined his scrotum I found it red and oedematous containing a tender and swollen right testicle. He told me it did not seem as painful as it had for the two days before. This was bad news if my diagnosis of a torsion (twisting) of the testicle were correct. In this condition, the testicle, for some unexplained reason, becomes twisted on its supporting vessels and so causes a constriction of the blood flow both ways, thus causing swelling and pain. It is more commonly found in horsemen than in other occupations. The fact that the pain got easier after a few days indicated some death of tissue, which was bad news. Oh, how I wished for my surgical colleague. I had to do something.

I put him in hospital immediately, closed the surgery and got Toby Barton for an anaesthetic.

When I opened up the scrotum, sure enough the right testicle was completely twisted through 360°. It was not difficult to untwist it, but waiting for signs of recovery of the circulation was the testing time. The testicle was twice its normal size and whether it was 'alive' or not would take some time to decide. If it had been twisted and strangulated too long it would be 'dead' and better removed. This was too big a decision for me. I could only hope it would recover. In my dilemma, not being able to decide about its viability, I decided to leave it after putting in a couple of holding sutures to stop it twisting again. Then I closed the scrotal incision and prayed!

He subsequently had a fever for a couple of days but the swelling and pain subsided. Two months later he was happy and grateful for what I had done, while I was thankful to my Managing Director above.

Walter returned, refreshed and ready to get going again and so began some of the happiest years of my medical life.

March came along. I, very courageously, spent a day in Sydney choosing a fur cape for RM's twenty-first birthday present and off I went to Adelaide by air. The trip from Sydney took six hours, stopping at Wagga, Narrandera, Hay, Mildura and Renmark before landing at Parafield.

My darling Rosemarie was there, slim and lovely. And so began two weeks of great happiness.

CHAPTER FOUR

The Jilted Lady

Our two weeks together passed all too quickly. As a prospective husband I had to be quizzed by many relatives of RM's family whose roots in South Australia dated from 1838. As a product of that large convict state, very much suspect by South Australians, I had to be examined in depth. Whatever my score in these examinations, the engagement was allowed to proceed. RM and I were now able to get to know something about each other, whilst her friends observed the old man (I was eleven years older than she) who had 'conned' her into living in the convict state. A memorable fortnight concluded by RM losing her pants—not as some readers will have by now anticipated—but by a button failure on the waist band of her laced satin scanties, fashionable in those days, as we walked down the steps of the South Australian Hotel after our last dinner there before my departure.

Back to Sydney by the usual six kangaroo hops of the Australian National Airways DC3 flight found me at my mother's home in Rose Bay, where I tried to convey to her that RM really would be a suitable wife for her little Leslie. They would not meet till June.

My happiness on return to country practice was translated into a spring in my step as I moved around the many home visits which seemed to be a part of every morning's activities. Hospital rounds, with two early morning operating sessions on Tuesdays and Wednesdays, and the afternoon consults in a temporary surgery built on to Walter's existing rooms, laid the foundations for a relationship between two souls

... concluded by RM losing her pants

who shared the same empathy for the general practitioner role in a country town. When I looked back to my existence of a few months earlier, I found it almost impossible to understand my good fortune. Walter and I fitted in perfectly as partners, his wife accepted me in their home and I had my future marriage to occupy much of my thinking.

Rosemarie was invited by the Pyes to come to Scone to survey the scene and would do so in June. There were many preparations on my part to prepare the nest. I bought a block of land and had a Sydney architect friend up to discuss plans for our home. As well as this Walter had many plans for us to build a new surgery complex separate from 'Waawaarawaa'. We bought land for this purpose and spent much time drawing up most detailed plans of what we wanted, and driving a local builder into feverish activity.

Our enterprise consisted of a large well furnished waiting room with the receptionist's office, records and accounts section, telephone area and appointment books, leading from it. Three consulting rooms, with attached examination rooms, all surrounded a large working room for a sister who would live in. Lots of minor procedures could be done here. An X-ray room, with our own film developing section and plaster room we felt was essential to save the innumerable trips we made to the Scott Memorial Hospital for all our fracture work. The sister's residence was connected at the rear via a tea room.

We had all this operating by the end of 1946, in spite of the innumerable difficulties in getting even the simplest of building materials and fittings. Rationing of essential materials within that first post-war year made building extremely difficult.

As time progressed I found myself being accepted by the people of Scone, probably because I was so closely associated with their beloved Walter. I was thus able to take quite a load off his shoulders as I was allowed to do more and more of the basic jobs. All the midwifery was now channelled my way which seemed to be quite acceptable to the ladies of Scone. I organised one afternoon a week for antenatal appointments, which gave Walter a free afternoon, while the surgery and waiting room was cluttered with mothers to be and mothers who had been. I was caring for about 120 births a year at that stage. Our staff liked this idea.

Many of the country calls came my way so that I learnt about the roads and the creeks at first hand.

Some calls were more eventful than others. I was getting excited about RM's coming visit which was only a short time away now, when Sergeant Bedingfield caught me at the mail box one morning and asked me to accompany him to the high country behind Ellerston station 70 miles north-east of Scone. He had a call earlier from the owner's wife who said there had been trouble in the shearing shed where some crutching was being done. The sergeant thought he should have a doctor along with him, so off we went with a constable driver. The road was long, seventy miles of it, winding, with many potholes and creek crossings. After much rain these trips were never possible, leaving owners isolated often for days.

I stuck around in the car while the sergeant and his constable made their investigations. Sure enough there had been some shooting. One chap had a massive gun-shot blast to his abdomen which wasn't pretty. He was beyond help. Another chap, lying in a corner, had some cuts and bruises about his forearms and face and neck; nothing really serious needing no more than some first aid bandages. Apparently he had made some statement to Sergeant Bedingfield, who told me he would have to take him back to town for questioning. He also decided to take the other body, stiffening up somewhat as we struggled to get him on to the back seat.

So there we were, now at nightfall, with one stiffening body, one with handcuffs and the three of us and the Ford car.

We all got in and called at the homestead to find the owner's wife and the housemaid wondering what had happened. Her husband had gone up to the high country the day before, with a team to muster cattle and was not expected home till the next day.

She showed the usual kindness to me and the sergeant by dispensing some whisky and suggested we stay for dinner as it was almost ready.

'How many of you are there?'

'Five in all, but it's a bit tricky' explained the sergeant.

'No that's no trouble, Edith will set the places, you bring them in'.

'No, I don't think we can do that'.

'Oh, don't be so silly, it's no bother' insisted our hostess.

'No, we really can't all come in, you see one is dead, Harry, I think his name is, or was, and Lenny I have handcuffed to my constable'.

'Oh dear' said our hostess, 'that's horrible. What are you going to do? Would you like one of our utilities to help you get back to town?'

'No, thank you so much, because you see three of us are unable to drive, so I think we had all better go in the one vehicle'.

'Well, you and the doctor had better have a bite and another whisky before you go, you certainly must need it'.

So, how was that for a trip? Sergeant Bedingfield drove, I was in front, Harry, in the middle of the back seat, to keep him upright, with the constable on one side of him and Lenny on the other. For safety's sake Lenny had been handcuffed to his dead victim. That seventy miles in the dark and the rain needs no further description, just imagination! It was early morning when we arrived at the hospital to deposit the corpse in the morgue, and Lenny, after some treatment, to a cell in the police station.

Toby Barton was the coroner's doctor so he would have his autopsy duties later in the day.

A country GP's life was much more exciting than that of his city brother, even though these adventures were never rewarded financially. However, they did assure the doctor of almost complete immunity from local problems, as well as, in this case, an assurance that RM would be granted her driving licence when she would be tested by the sergeant.

This adventure really appealed to Walter when I related it next day. He had a wonderful sense of humour, always quick to appreciate the comic in any situation, as well as a quirky imagination. Together we contemplated the situation if Sergeant Bedingfield had accepted the offer of a utility. Would I have been asked to drive that while he stuck to the police car? Would I have the body or the accused? If I had the body it would have to be in the front rather than out in the heavy rain. How would I have kept it upright? No seat belts had been thought of in the '40s, so it may have cuddled up to me — ugh! The creeks were rising fast and Omadale Brook was steep and deep with a well known reputation for catching daring and frustrated drivers who attempted it, often carrying vehicles away down stream. Should I then try to save the body, a necessary part of a murder trial—no body, no murder? Would I be equal to the task?

If on the other hand, I had been asked to take the accused with me in the utility and the creek caught us, would I be able to prevent his escape into the hills and disappear? No, we agreed, I should have the body, this was the doctor's job, the police should guard the criminal.

So we rambled on, with Walter contorting himself and stamping his foot on the floor, which I had seen so often, as he imagined each new situation. He was delightful. Our appreciation of situations could always be tuned closely, which meant we had the greatest delight in each other's company, even while operating deep in the abdomen we often had our laughs. Not all days were gay (I use this word in its correct sense) there were many problem days with little humour to be found at the time.

This adventure, to the murder scene at Barrington Tops, had another quirky turn, which partly helped me solve a difficult situation which was becoming awkward, to say the least.

During 1940, the year I had in Scone before going off to war, I had received quite a lot of attention from a young lady, the inheritor-to-be, of one of the great sheep grazing properties in this district. She had been well educated in Sydney and in Switzerland and had charms which had not, to that time, brought the dividend of matrimony. The young bachelor doctor was worth pursuing. The prospect of war relieved me of any serious decision in 1940, but on my return, still without her dividend, I was set up for a takeover.

Her parents were rather old and most conservative; the apple of their eye had been a late arrival, and unfortunately, the only one for this magnificent inheritance.

I believe I must have been considered fairly suitable as the future squire because I had been sought in Sydney immediately upon my return from prison camps. I looked like being caught at this time, in my quite defenceless state, with scalp hair just beginning to grow, my skin yellow with the massive doses of atebrin, my weight very much lower than was normal for me, as was my resistance. I was feted in the most lavish fashion and almost fell for the proposal. Something held me back. I never did know quite what, for the rewards were great. The proposals became a little aggressive, which scared me a bit and decided me to drive to Adelaide to see my sister, whose attractions were calling. This was not well received by the jumbuck empire.

Bad luck! because within a week I had met Rosemarie, whose attractions won, even without the inheritance.

Love is still quite a mystery to me. Why should I have chosen RM and faced a life in which I would have to earn security, when that of the land, littered with Rolls Royces, was on the plate? Our decision was quick and has proved itself over forty years. It is probably only that little boy in Piccadilly Circus, with his quiver full, who controls their destination.

My return to practice in Scone early in 1946 was not without this festering social situation. My engagement in Adelaide had not been announced so I thought it was quite a secret.

I was quickly asked to the estate for dinner. Father and mother were most attentive, though the daughter!!! . . . I was not sure. Had she suspected, or had she even heard of the engagement?

I think I must have been deliberately naughty at the dinner table for I brought up the subject of my recent adventure to the murder at Ellerston and described how Walter and I had enjoyed our literal post-mortem of its amusing side. The subject was not well received by conservative Mum and Dad. I had made my social faux pas . . . at last.

After the repast we were left alone on the spacious verandah surrounded by the splendour of the silver coffee service and the brandy decanter, gazing across the moonlit countryside, dotted with thousands of four-legged money boxes, when I was reprimanded for my faux pas! This was the first time I had seen her like this!!

Just then, my one false tooth, a front incisor on a midget dental plate, got stuck in my chocolate toffee and dislodged itself into the centre of my mouth. Fearing I might swallow it, I made a sudden embarrassing departure from the peaceful scene. This was completely misinterpreted which provoked the heiress to lose her cool and say . . . 'If I were married to you I'd kill you . . . I'd poison your coffee'.

I laughed, which I should not have done, but I felt relieved as I saw the affair ending. I also thought of Winston Churchilll's retort to Nancy Astor, who once said this same thing to him. His well known quip was . . . 'And if I were married to you, I'd drink it'.

CHAPTER FIVE

The Baby Competition

I was quite happy that this one-sided romance had ended without real bloodshed although I still had an inner sort of feeling that there may be some repercussion . . . one day.

My heart was bright and gay as I went about my work in the next few days. My thoughts kept dashing back to Adelaide and my darling RM. I was off guard, I suppose, when Mrs Payne came in to see me on an afternoon consult. A little strange, as she usually saw Walter and had done so for many a year. My ego was tickled I suppose, for I knew Walter was also in the surgery doing a consult. Anyway I didn't have to think of this for long when she told me she had come to see me about one of her daughters who had recently married and become pregnant. She wanted to discuss the pros and cons of her being looked after by me in my antenatal service and whether she should have her baby in Scone or in the 'big smoke'. So I realised why she had come to see me. My ego slipped back a notch.

My defences were down when she opened up the other reason for her visit to me. Mrs Payne was the President of the Country Women's Associaton of the Upper Hunter. She went on to tell me that the Moonan Sub-branch was having a fete in four weeks time on a Saturday. It was to be the usual sort of country town affair to raise money from the sale of jams, cakes, pickles, and ever so many more home produced goodies. Carnival events had been arranged for all ages from the children upwards so it all seemed well organised. There would be prizes for the competition winners as usual. This year, she went on to tell me, she wanted to introduce something new now that the war was over and people could 'let their hair down' and really enjoy the day.

She put her idea to me, which I did not appreciate fully at the time. Her idea was to introduce a baby show and competition, with a first, second and third prize. Would I be the judge? This shook me quite a bit. Why should I be asked when there were others, much more experienced than I, such as Toby Barton or Walter, my partner? My ego had a resurgence. Being the young doctor, back from the war, I was eager to be well received and accepted again in this great country community. 'Yes, of course, I would be only too happy to help'. But I did add that I had never done anything like this before and hoped I would be equal to the task. Mrs Payne was sure I would be just the one for the job and mentioned that the district sister at Moonan, Miss Thistlewaite, would be in charge of all the arrangements and there would be no problem for me. All I would be required to do would be to judge the babies and afterwards to say just a few words and announce the prizewinners. It all sounded so easy that I did not appreciate the pitfalls of such an assignment.

At afternoon tea I mentioned this to Walter who seemed very happy that I had been invited by Mrs Payne to do this. With a twinkle in his eye he said how much I would enjoy it, and went on to talk about some of his many patients from Moonan. It was a very small outpost in the upper reaches of the Hunter River, whose water and soils were renowned for their lack of iodine.

'Some of the old families there are quite "funny", he said, an expression he often used when talking about, and educating me about, some of the people in our district whom he had got to know most intimately, as their confidant. I can hear him, even now, so often saying—'they're funny doctor; very funny'. He was a kind man yet this saying of his was always so appropriate. It described the subject in a way no other words could. I had the feeling that he had once been asked to judge a baby show.

I had a month to think about this exciting event though I admit it was not uppermost in my thoughts. My work and RM were always number one. Sister Batterham said to me one morning at 'Brancaster', 'I hear you are going to judge the baby show at Moonan'.

'Yes, tell me how to judge one baby from another' was my plea, for I could not think of a better person to ask.

'Oh', she said, 'just use your own feelings, but have a good look at the mothers first and keep your eye on them when you are judging their babies'.

I couldn't really understand why she stressed this aspect of judging a baby show, but I would remember what she said.

As the time drew near I really began to think about some standards I should adopt. I was told all the babies would be aged from birth to six months, older ones were not eligible.

Would I judge them on weight, that is weight for age? This seemed to me a fairly reasonable measurement. It would make a judgment on the health of the baby generally; whether it was putting on weight by absorbing its food as well as it should be—according to the well recognised tables we used in those days.

This brought up the thorny question of whether the baby had been breast fed or bottle fed, always a contentious question even in a dairying district. Was this why 'Batt' had asked me to have a good look at the mothers? I had a pretty open mind about feeding methods, or put more accurately, I had an empty mind on the subject. So I rather dismissed this as being an important measurement for a prize.

Would the baby's length be an appropriate standard to use? Again I could see many traps in this. Not only should I keep my eyes on the mother, but surely the father's genes would play their part in determining the length of any offspring. Keep an eye on father too!

Did sex play any part? Of course it did — why hadn't Mrs Payne arranged for a separate competition for boys and girls? This, I thought would be much fairer. I always had, and still have, a soft spot for girls and I could clearly recognise a sex discrimination (very modern thinking in 1946) if weight and length were to be used as judging standards. If Mrs Payne had organised a male and female section I certainly could have had an accurate measurement to sort out one boy from another. The graziers of the district were beginning to use the 'scrotal measurement' as a scientific selection method. Or, could I? On reflection, I realised this portion of the anatomy in those so young could not sensibly be included in my judging methods. There seemed no other sexual aspects that I could consider in those under six months of age.

Perhaps there was. Should circumcision be mentioned? Would a boy have an advantage if he were circumcised? The pitfalls here were also obvious. After all, the decision to have a circumcision could have been made by either the doctor or the parents. This made any judgment on this question also pretty unscientific.

While debating about this area of the newborn, I reminded myself of a great indiscretion I once made in my pre-war year of 1940 when I didn't know my patients very well. I had just delivered a baby without any difficulty when I was asked by the big burly farmer father, who was expecting a boy as a future tractor driver—'Is the baby all right doctor?'

'Yes', I told him 'screamed its head off straightaway and it's pink and healthy'. I went on, in my stupidly flippant way to say, 'but it has been born without a penis'.

'Oh my God' said the farmer 'that's dreadful, what can be done about that?'

'Well, I wouldn't let it bother you too much just at present. There's a lovely little place where one can be put later on'. It took quite a while for his anxious expression to melt away.

So much for sex!

I thought of so many other possible ways to judge one baby against another. The ones who screamed at me when I would lift them up, would be marked down — so I would use temperament as a yardstick. If the mothers couldn't control them better than that, then they would suffer. I could feel myself floundering as I tried to get some firm yardsticks for my judgments.

Did hair, or the lack of it, mean anything, did blue eyes beat brown eyes, would the presence of a couple of lower incisor teeth influence me at all?

What about presentation, upon which judges at dog shows were so insistent? Could I use this? Would I include the cot as well as the clothes? Surely this would discriminate against the mother's ability to sew or knit or even her buying power.

Within a few days of this wretched event I began to hope I would come down with measles or some even worse catastrophe in order to justify my escape from this trap which Walter and Toby and 'Batt' were all by now beginning to enjoy, as my predicament was making me a nervous wreck, quite unreliable and irritable in the surgery.

I became a complete squib until I thought of the answer. Why didn't I ask 'Batt' to come out with me to Moonan and be my assistant, to keep the score as I advanced from one worm to another, after all, she could whisper pearls in my ear as I kept my eyes on the mothers, which she was so insistent on my doing.

'Batt' put on her wise smile and told me how sorry she was. She had given her nurse-aide the week-end off to go to Sydney for her sister's wedding, an event that could not be put off for a baby show. She tried to reassure me I would be all right once I got there, as long as I kept smiling and nodding and said very little. 'Keep watching the mothers', she repeated.

The dreaded day came, sunny and beautiful in autumn, after good rains. This, I thought, should make everybody happy in the bush township and even forgiving, if I erred in my judgment.

Not a bit of it—Mrs Payne greeted me with her confident motherly smile as she led me to meet the Moonan district nurse, Miss Thistle-waite, in her middle age. She smiled and said how happy she was that I had come and looked forward to an interesting competition. Interesting for whom?—I thought. I was led into the main school hall (or was it my slaughterhouse) full of bassinets and cots and was reasonably quiet at 11.30 am. The ten o'clock feeds had all been given—one way or the other—so comfort reigned.

The mothers, standing alongside their entrants, glared at me as I kept my exaggerated smile in place. I was determined not to be rattled.

I did have a chance, as Mrs Payne left me, to get a few words regarding my fears into Miss Thistlewaite, and even asked her for her help. She said she would do all she could to help me, but I had to realise that she lived amongst all these mothers and babies, and that it would be more than her life was worth to be heard or seen to influence me in any way at all. This would have to be very strictly observed. I was the 'bunny'.

The judging began, pencil and note-pad in my hand. As I was introduced to each mother and then looked at her offering, placed my hand on the head, looked in the mouth when possible, without upsetting the comfort of the recent feed, felt the muscle tone, examined the hip joints for signs of congenital dislocation, a condition incidentally that can easily be overlooked until the child gets to walking age and looked for the proper complement of fingers and toes, I found my mind becoming more and more confused. Then I suddenly had the bright idea—why had I not thought of this before—it would have saved many sleepless nights. I suddenly realised one measurement I could make that could not be challenged. I would use my staff of office, I would listen to each baby's heart and lungs with my stethoscope. This gave me much needed confidence, for now I was able to pass from one cot to the other, using different facial expressions, and making unintelligible mutterings as I made my notes, taking care to avoid speaking to Miss Thistlewaite on any occasion, so as she would not be involved with my decisions.

Unbeknownst to my large audience I was coming to the conclusion that I hadn't the faintest idea of what I was doing, nor were my notes in any way recording any sensible judgments. However my stethoscope carried me through, even though, by now, it was completely impossible to hear anything through the tubes for the considerable screaming I had provoked by my examinations. It seemed to me they were all beginning to wonder what time the next feed would come along.

How on earth would I finish this charade? I remembered watching an equestrian event at the Scone show on a previous occasion and learnt that the judge, in complete silence, and alone, pulled six horses and riders into the centre of the ring for final judgment. I would do something similar. I walked along all the cots and touched every sixth one, as there were about 30 competitors, and asked them to take centre ring.

This masterstroke was greeted with some undercurrent rumblings which I thought may be a forerunner of violence later on. However, swinging my stethoscope from the nuchal position, I appeared confident, still smiling, as I gazed at the six on my short list.

At this stage I tore out the pages from my notebook, with my scribblings so far, rolled them up and put them firmly in my trouser pocket. They would be safe there from those maternal eyes.

I started a new page as I re-examined the six. I found I had three boys and three girls, as well as twelve parents standing alongside their respective entrants. This I thought would be the moment 'Batt' had mentioned when I should keep a close eye on the mothers. She hadn't mentioned the fathers, who I thought, looked far more foreboding—except perhaps for one particular woman!

Again I felt their muscle tone and looked at their personalities and their presentations. The only possible way I could now decide first, second and third was to use the parents.

Realising I could be lynched, I chose the winning baby whose parents were the smallest. So too the second and third. All these parents looked harmless enough, and I thought, by now all the other parents would be exhausted with nervous tension, as was the judge.

So I now approached Miss Thistlewaite for the first time since the judging began, quickly putting my notebook in my pocket, without showing her my 'methods', and said I was ready to announce the prize-winners. She could just hear me for the din I had started in the school hall, all of which I thought would be to my advantage, because any remarks I intended to make would probably not be heard.

Miss Thistlewaite introduced me and I took the stand on the box provided. News must have spread that the judging was now over and the doctor would announce the winners and present the prizes, for the hall seemed much fuller now.

With the blue, red and green ribbons over my forearm and after a few opening remarks, with the smile still in place, I congratulated all the mothers who had entered such a fine field of competitors. I explained how difficult it had been to make my judgments even though I had used modern scientific methods, very newly discovered. There should be no feeling of disappointment for those who were not chosen, just as there should be no over excitement among those who got prizes. The decisions were among the most difficult I had ever made, but the judge's choices must be accepted. I then distributed the ribbons and the prizes to the winners.

Just as I thought I was getting away with the whole show, that one mother, who had been regarding me with a most aggressive look during the whole hour and a half, spoke up and said, 'A fine judge you are—we all know the baby with the first prize has a cleft palate'.

As Miss Thistlewaite showed me quickly to my car she told me my aggressor was a cousin of the young lady whose advances I had recently spurned. I always suspected there would be a repercussion from the rejection of this young lady but little did I expect it from this quarter. Moonan might have been a small town but it didn't miss out on much news. Those manual telephone exchanges were far more lethal than the modern efforts at phone tapping.

It was quite apparent I had failed. I returned to Scone a much wiser man!

CHAPTER SIX

Manipulative Arts

Childbirth has proved itself to be one of the most lasting of all human activities. There is no need to study the Egyptian papyri, nor those of Babylon, China or Peru to be convinced of this. Just look around.

Two things should interest us about childbirth.

The first is that only in this present generation, of all those that have passed, have the difficulties of childbirth been conquered. Today, at last, no woman in our developed societies need suffer a difficult birth. The safety of Caesarean section delivery is well known. Although this is a very old operation, recorded in the Egyptian papyri, it was only done in an attempt to save the life of the baby after the mother's death. Today both lives are saved.

The second; is to be reminded of the multitude of methods adopted to deliver reluctant babies.

There are recordings in these old papyri that in a normal birth the child's head should always come first. It was recognised that there were many abnormal presentations, such as an arm or a foot or even cross presentations. Locked twins, like many other problems, were recognised and recorded.

When labour began, progress was watched by midwives of those times. Our interest begins when progress was delayed. What did they do?

Thinking that the child needed some incentive to be born, it was the custom to prepare an attractive meal, served on a plate and placed at the entrance of the birth canal. Some of the older Egyptian and Babylonian midwives built their reputations on secret recipes. What a pity the details of these culinary attractions have never yet been discovered!

After failure to achieve any progress by this method the records show that various forms of incense would be offered. The prescription for these fumigants varied enormously, some exotic, some objectionable depending upon the experiences and teachings of the midwives.

The commonest position during labour and delivery was undoubtedly the squatting or sitting position. Many illustrations, throughout the centuries, show these as the commonest. Sometimes the prospective mother would be supported from behind; the assistant with her arms around the swollen belly endeavouring to help squeeze the child out.

An infinite list of drugs and potions shows they had been concocted to aid in childbirth, to drive out demons and exorcists.

With the development of surgical skills, even in the stone age, instruments were made to extract reluctant children. With the onset of the bronze and iron age, many different sorts of hooks and other instruments were fashioned to aid childbirth.

These early attempts to help difficult childbirths are well recorded and make exciting reading for those of us who entered this arena of medicine.

When I entered it the manipulative arts were highly developed. Instruments had been perfected not only for aiding the delivery of the baby's head but for turning it into the most suitable position before using traction. There were instruments for aiding breech presentations as well as those for enlarging the size of the bony pelvis by the use of the operation of symphysiotomy.

Destructive instruments, of many different kinds, were available for piecemeal delivery of a dead baby which was too large to be manipulated in any other way.

I witnessed, with wonder, the dexterity of my senior tutors performing many of these manipulative arts while in residence at my obstetric teaching hospital in 1936 and 1937.

As students in residence we witnessed these complicated births, while being trained in the art of conducting a normal delivery. Each of us was required to deliver twenty babies. We learnt the after care of the mother and even the baby, which was entrusted to us. We put silver nitrate drops in its eyes, tied off the cord and took it to the nursery and gave it its first bath. This was essential before each of us could be credited with his twenty deliveries.

At this early stage of my medical career I was attracted to the excitements of childbirth, but soon tired of baby bathing. I made an arrangement with a group colleague, Bill Marsh, to pay him 3d to wash each of my babies. This cheating, which crept into my training, was understood by the nursery sister, who earned a box of chocolates for her 'blind' eye. Bill loved babies and should have gone on to be a paediatrician.

As a student one could but watch the more complicated procedures of a forceps delivery, a breech delivery or a manual removal of a placenta. It was probably at this stage of our careers, in the latter years of our training, that those of us who were basically carpenters at heart, developed the yearning to do what we watched our surgical or our obstetric teachers doing. There seemed to be a great satisfaction in doing something which needed doing, and which required training to do it satisfactorily. We recognised that further post-graduate training would be necessary before we would have this satisfaction. Before this could be done, there was something else that needed doing.

Nineteen-thirty-nine to nineteen-forty-five were not years for obstetric training. That would have to wait. However they were not wasted years. They gave us a training of a greater and different kind.

In the earlier years of the century it was not customary for medical graduates to undertake post-graduate training. Few specialties had been developed. Most young doctors entered general practice and undertook what came along. If they felt incapable of handling some problem in a city practice they could always refer the case to a public hospital. The more adventurous ones, who preferred practice in the country, rarely had help close at hand when in difficulties and therefore often had to improvise.

There was a country doctor at Nyngan in NSW, in 1916, who knew the baby had died in a difficult and long labour and who had no forceps to apply to the head to try to pull it down. He tried the old pepper trick which made the woman sneeze violently without the desired effect. He then did what he had seen farmers do with their cows. He was able to get a rope up around the baby's neck. Not very nice, alas, but he did get it out. Those days are no longer.

There was a young doctor in Scone, early in 1946, soon after he returned to practice from the war years, who was faced with a tightly fitting head, causing the tired mother great difficulty in pushing it out.

'It's no good' said Sister Batterham 'you'll have to use the forceps'.

'I've never used them 'Batt', surely we can wait a little longer', I said quietly, hoping the mother didn't hear.

'She's been in labour for 24 hours, and I'm sure she's too tired now to push it any further. You must put the forceps on or the baby will die'.

I knew what to do. I had read it up only a short time ago thinking this would happen. The left blade had to be inserted first otherwise they would not lock. I knew how to pick the left blade from the right. I also knew I would have to go ahead and do it.

'Batt' was quite safe with the chloroform. She had been, for forty years. Would I be safe with the forceps?

I put the mother's legs in the stirrups, draped her and then a confidence came over me. I was no longer nervous. I could see the baby's head and I had ingseen this done before. I would do it and get the baby out.

All went well with the application. The blades went on easily and I had remembered to empty the mother's bladder.

Now, a gentle pull. No progress, I would have to pull harder.

'What are you doing under the bed?' I heard 'Batt' say.

God, what a fool I was.

After washing the mother by splashing the Dettol solution liberally about, the smooth ironite floor with the rubber mat was so wet that as I leaned backwards to pull on the forceps the mat took off, with me on

board. We went in under the bed. I had, of course, let the handle of the forceps go, so I didn't take them and the baby as well! The forceps were locked firmly round the baby's head.

Up and redraped, I tried again, this time with one foot firmly placed against one leg of the bed. With a little persuasion and a rocking motion . . .

'It's coming 'Batt'.

'Good. Don't hurry it now. Watch that perineum. As soon as you're ready, tell me and I'll stop the chloroform'.

'Yes, OK. One more pull and I reckon the head will be born. Now: take off the mask'.

And so all ended well. The baby didn't suffer. The mother never knew I fell under the bed. I would have to do some post-graduate training when I got a chance.

When Walter returned I told him of my 'slip'.

'Doctor, I've done it twice on that slippery floor. Always put your foot on the end of the bed'.

I had very good reason to remember the floor of that room. Not because I was injured in any way. I was young and healthy and didn't injure easily. It was not even the feeling of embarrassment that ensured its place in my memories. None of these things.

It was the room in which I first practised some of the many obstetric procedures I had seen done by my tutors. There was the first time I had the audacity to invade the sanctity of the womb to separate an adherent placenta (afterbirth) in order to control that most fearsome bogey of post-partum haemorrhage. My feelings today are almost as vivid as they were then in that little room. I had to do it—'Batt' said so. Could I do it? Would my separating fingers puncture the uterine wall? I was quite unsure and quite untrained for this responsibility. I had no tutor watching over me. My gods looked over me. Whether I did it as well as the many hundreds I had done since, I have no idea. But what I did, stopped the haemorrhage. I well remember the loneliness my hand felt, trying to do the right thing, as I gazed into 'Batt's' eyes watching me from the head end of the bed.

The many other manipulations I did for the first time in that little room; the first internal version, the first impacted breech and others, make that little room, second on the right down the front hall, one of the most sacred places on earth to me.

'Batt's' instinct and guidance not only encouraged me in that field of medicine but have been closely behind me ever since. She died many years ago—with the passing of these manipulative arts. No one today learns, practises or even needs them. Caesarean section is the panacea for all these problems.

There is no sadness here. The increased safety of our first and loneliest voyage surely compensates for the loss of these exciting and challenging manipulations.

CHAPTER SEVEN

Nuptials and So To Bed

The last week in June arrived, as did Rosemarie. I went down to Mascot Airport to meet the kangaroo-hopping DC3, and an exhausted RM. The meeting, between the two most important women, in my life, would shortly take place in my mother's house at Rose Bay.

RM was wearing a cherry red overcoat with a matching beret, a little down over her right eye. Her hair was short and I thought she looked tired. She was quieter than I had expected. I wondered why. Was it just tiredness or was she having 'second thoughts'? Perhaps the sudden realisation of what marrying into the great convict state would mean, was on her mind. How does one ever know what is 'on the mind' of intelligent women?

I had always thought how brave girls, and young women were when they agreed to a marriage proposal. What a decision to make! Probably the greatest they would ever make. It meant leaving home, their parents, their friends and all their past, if a major move were involved. The young lady would agree to leave all the comforts, or at least the status quo of her present life, for the great unexpected; the new world of her husband. What a risk!! Would he be kind, would he be generous, would he look after her, or would it all be a disaster?

These thoughts may have been in her mind and accounted for her quietness. How did I know? Women are much braver than men in these situations. I do not believe men would be as composed if the situation were reversed. They would not face such an upheaval of their life-style with this feminine courage.

Mater, as Rosemarie was to call her, was then seventy-one years of age, but the features, so admired in her younger years, were still attractive. At the turn of the century, she was considered as one of Sydney's beauties; average height, the compulsory wasp waist, a cloud of red gold hair, with beautifully set hazel eyes. She was lucky enough to have had dark lashes and eyebrows, without the freckles, which usually accompanied this colouring. Time had changed her, but not the basics.

The meeting was mutually cautious. The two women were making their judgments. One just twenty-one the other, fifty years older. The older one suspicious, as all mothers are when first meeting a prospective daughter-in-law, the younger one, intelligent enough to handle any situation.

'She's not what I expected, which makes me happy. Some of those pretty girls you used to bring home, before the war, often seemed a bit 'flighty'. This one is so sensible and intelligent. She seemed so tired last night, but this morning, I really see what an attractive girl she is. She is young and quietly confident and speaks beautifully. She will be a good doctor's wife and I feel sure you will be happy together. You both have my blessing and wishes for a long life together'.

These were Mater's comments to me, while RM had gone walking to the nearest post box with a letter to her parents.

For two days we had a quick look around the Sydney shops, doing a reconnaissance. There would be much to buy later on, but for now, just a gift for Gwen, who had invited her to have a look around Scone.

RM did not intend to stay long. The house site and the plans, soon to be put into action, were exciting. Thoughts about furniture and curtains and the numerous ideas and decisions were eagerly discussed. While Walter and I had busy days, RM went walking and did her own surveys. The visit was all too short, but most essential for RM who would go back to Adelaide, knowing where her future lay, and what would be needed, while she prepared for the wedding in September.

Whilst driving RM down the 200 miles to Sydney, a strange and most fortunate thing happened. Two hours after we left Scone, Walter was contacted by the estate agent who told him of a large house, about to be sold, which he thought would suit the young couple. On our arrival at Mater's house we were greeted with the news. We accepted our good fortune, for the building of our own house could never have been ready for us by September, which meant a long stint in a hotel—not a happy prospect. Of course I would buy it. A pity we had not known of it two hours earlier for then we could have seen it. As it was, RM would now have to have plans and measurements sent on to her in Adelaide.

The many preliminary parties given her by her friends all lacked the bridegroom, until a few days before the wedding date, when he appeared.

At 3 pm on 18 September 1946 our wedding took place at Christ Church, North Adelaide, before the many guests who later went on to the reception in Rosemarie's own home, where she was born and brought up. It was a gay affair.

Our sleeping arrangements were the subject of some anxiety in the early few days of our married life, probably more so for me than for RM. We had been given the use of a delightful cottage in the hills near Stirling for a week as a wedding present from a friend of RM's mother. A most peaceful existence, all on our own, with a house stuffed with asparagus and champagne, had only one drawback as far as RM could see. It had a double bed!!

Now the question of a double bed had never entered my head. I saw my mother and father sleep in a double bed and, no doubt, throughout my growing years, I had unconsciously accepted the reality that married people slept in double beds. In the last few years I mostly slept on the ground or on some makeshift contraption acting as a bed so, you see I never gave this subject any detailed thought. Sufficient, when I returned to a humane society, was any bed at all. I did expect a mattress and bed-clothes, and a hot water bottle on cold nights, which I automatically thought would be replaced by something much more cuddlesome, certainly after marriage, and had often considered, but always unsuccessfully, before marriage. My thoughts were therefore rather simple and basic and obviously had been neglected. Not so RM's. Just how much thought she had given this subject was never really discussed. Did young girls, about to be married, talk about these subjects or was the thinking done in private? How would I, a mere husband, ever know the process which led to the statement—'We are not going to sleep in a double bed'.

This was a stunning blow to me—how serious was she—what was the alternative? Was there going to be a 'disaster' on the first night of our honeymoon? I had heard of such happenings but really had no idea what was meant, nor had I ever given it much thought—till now!!!

In fact one of my pre-war girl friends married a well known Australian sporting chap in 1944 and when I came home I was told she left him the day after the wedding. This was well known, but I never did learn the reason. How could this occur? I found it incredible. What could have happened or what could they have found out about each other to result in two 'sensible' people going, so emphatically, to the divorce court? I seem to have heard of this happening on other occasions, but what shocked me was that I knew these two. I thought I did. Surely this could never happen to us!!

I looked around the house. There were two other bedrooms with a single bed in each, all beautifully made up with decorative flowers all over the house. This was a wonderful wedding present.

I began to wonder what our situation would have been had we decided to spend our first night together in a room in the South Australian Hotel. Had I not stipulated two single beds and RM found a double bed in the bridal chamber, what would she then do? Would there have been a scene and a call for the manager? Not in Adelaide, surely.

I decided to take matters in hand by opening a bottle of champagne and a tin of asparagus; a mixture we always enjoyed, especially with the encore. The fire was burning nicely, the lights were out, which all resulted in our sleeping in each other's arms, on the couch, until 3 am. Getting married was a strenuous business. We woke at mid-morning—in the double bed. We had survived. All my imaginings were unnecessary.

Young married couples, and even others, young and old, do agree there are occasions when it is pleasant to occupy the same mattress and bedclothes, but RM convinced me that somnolent perfection was only possible in one's own outfit.

I fell in with RM's wishes!! There would be no split. There would be 'consensus' in today's terms. In fact when I did begin to consider the question seriously I realised the wisdom of my twenty-one-year-old bride. For those who have not experienced life in a doctor's house it may be difficult to understand the bed situation. When a general practitioner becomes successful, he finds that he is forever on call to his patients, who may number from 2000 to 4000 in a country practice. I suppose some nights would pass without being wakened by a telephone call, but they would be in the minority. Maybe every call would not mean leaving the bed; advice may be all that was asked; but as the midwifery cases increase so do the disturbed nights.

'Who's that darling', in a very sleepy voice. 'Oh, it's 'Brancaster', Mrs Jones is ready for delivery'.

This, or a myriad of other reasons, meant the bed would have to be vacated. To get out of a double bed, without disturbing one's partner during the night, is probably just as impossible as it would be to enter a double bed without disturbing the prospective partner. I am guessing! In any case getting into bed from the freezing temperatures of the Upper Hunter, in winter time, would probably again raise the question of divorce.

No; RM was quite right. Separate beds for sleeping was the correct decision. They need not be separated by much, but they must have their own mattress and bed-clothes. As the years progress, and age takes its toll, this system of separate beds lends itself to easily adapted modifications. The distance between can be increased—little by little—with perhaps a table in between, until the bed in the adjoining room may even be used, especially if snoring becomes a problem. Many couples find other reasons for separate beds in later life, so if one starts on the correct path in the beginning, adjustments may be made most smoothly. Not, as I once heard a friend of my mother's tell her, when I was not meant to be listening—'Yes (sob—sob) he no longer sleeps in my bed'. This serious and traumatic step can be avoided if RM's dictum is followed, sic. 'We are not going to sleep in a double bed'.

After we left our idyllic cottage in the Adelaide Hills, where we seemed to be so tired that we would have slept whatever the situation, we found no hotels on our drive around the Great Ocean Road, in Melbourne or through NSW, which had appreciated my wife's wisdom. We had to suffer double beds. Only in later years, when motels arrived, did we see the beginning of civilised sleeping. Progresss was being made. RM was before her time.

Now, statistics show quite conclusively that double beds are associated with a much higher divorce rate than separate beds. As a scientist, I cannot accept any direct correlation between these two facts. Surely the question of who you are in bed with is more relevant than the size of the bed.

In late September two married couples arrived in Scone, on the same day, each to occupy their new homes. Sep Halliday, a solicitor who began practice in Scone before the war, as I had done, had married Betty Austin in 1944. She came from the merino country in Western NSW. Their new house was in Waverley Street, ours in Phillip Street.

'You'll have to sit on the polished pine boards which Les has just sanded and polished, and drink your gin from your own glasses as we only have two cups', explained RM, as she rang and asked the Halliday's to come around to celebrate this combined arrival in Scone, of the doctor and the solicitor.

'Sure, we'll be around pronto', said Betty as she got RM to agree to go and spill gin on their boards in Waverley Street before the day ended.

So began a happy and close friendship between the two couples.

All our early problems with beds would be over once we got our own furniture in Phillip Street. RM would be able to rule her own roost. Our furniture had not yet arrived. There were packing cases as well as a large collection of building materials scattered about as some alterations were yet to be completed. Our friends offered to help, but raised their eyebrows a little when RM requested two single mattresses. This request was granted, even though it was regarded as a little odd. 'Why don't they sleep together . . . has he been cruel to her . . . will the marriage last?' must have been some of their thoughts.

RM knew what she wanted. I had the difficult job of setting up packing cases, four in all, with sheets of masonite suspended between them, on which the mattresses were placed, and on which the beds eventually were made. The unevenness of the cases, placed for two beds, alongside each other, one sloping in an east-west direction, the other towards the equator, made for unstable outfits.

After our efforts with the Hallidays, when we emptied two bottles of gin, we wobbled home along Waverley Street in the Vauxhall, in low gear, for safety, and with a blood alcohol level, if such a thing had been thought of then, way up in the clouds.

We would sleep properly tonight, in separate beds. Rosemarie always took the one on the right—she still does, unless the left one has a softer mattress—so, with our clothes on the floor we got into our separate beds and slept exceedingly well, because of the gin.

This was the pattern of our bedroom for some few more days until our furniture arrived.

Without the gin our beds continually collapsed, not for the reason that some readers may imagine when young recent honeymooners retire on to insecure beds. No; that was not the reason for our insecurity. It was all to do with me.

Now that I had got out of the hands of the Japanese and got back to my own home I was looking forward to a peaceful existence. I found I began to dream. Several nights I encountered Japanese guards who had no right to be in my house and whom I would attempt to strangle—and once I almost did. I heard a faint cry—'Les, Les, let me go'—Poor RM.

CHAPTER EIGHT

Settling in to Social Life

Towards the end of 1946 I began to take stock of my life's situation. It seemed to be the first opportunity of its kind for many years. The university years were a preliminary to, but in no way a guarantee of, security. One had to struggle, quite hard in my case, to keep up with the stream I had started with in 1932. I was neither of distinction nor, except for once, of credit material among my hundred colleagues. Each year, for the whole six of them, it was a gamble. Would I still have time to continue with my lawn tennis and, in the end, to convince my examiners that I should be allowed over the annual hurdle? There was no peace for me in those years.

The short respite, after my eventual graduation, in two years at Royal Prince Alfred Hospital, was a sort of 'marking time', because of Hitler. We argued a lot, but I am sure now, we all thought the coming war forbade any future plans, and so added to our insecurity.

Bill Gailey and Bob Duval, my room mates would say, 'Oh, come on Ossie (my RPAH nickname), forget about the future, let's go over to the 'Lalla Rook' and have a pint or two'. A pint was a pint in Sydney in 1939, served in a tall sloping-sided glass, all for a shilling. With that came cheese and biscuits. With relaxation, came dinner in the residents dining room, always finishing with ice cream and chocolate sauce. This all helped, in a way, but looking ahead, the very immediate future may have involved a nurse's company, but beyond that—what would it be?

The next six years, whatever one did, set a course directly opposite to security and future planning.

Hoorah, hoorah! now in October 1946, for the first time ever in my life, which now extended to 32 years, I could see a future. My Rosemarie had shown faith in me, the war was over, and I was a junior partner, with Walter Pye, in a wonderful country practice. So it was time to take stock.

My assets were my wife, my house, my Vauxhall coupe, and my share of the partnership, which would be a 50% share, when I could afford the £500 remaining on the purchase price. The material assets, worth very little really, but with RM, always quietly confident, I felt security coming on.

In fact, looking back now (1986) on those forty years, I have no recollection of looking too far ahead, or of worrying too much about what the future held for me or where I would, or wanted to, end up. The final move, of course, was inevitable. That had been met, full on, many times in the last four years and had luckily been avoided. Of one thing I was certain, between now and that final move, which only the Domesday Book could reveal, every day would be considered a bonus. I was lucky to have survived, when so many of my earlier university colleagues and friends, had not.

So it was, on that late October day when I drove in for lunch, seeing the large van from Grace Brothers had already delivered our carpets and our furniture, which RM and Elsie were guiding into position, I felt complete security and consequently, great happiness.

'You must be Elsie' was RM's guess as this nineteen-year-old girl walked up to the kitchen door earlier that morning.

Elsie was the eldest child of a family living at Blandford, some 20 miles further north on the railway line towards Tamworth.

'Yes, I'm Elsie. My mother spoke to you about my taking this position of housemaid. She is a patient of the doctor's. You're his wife, I presume'?

'Yes, Elsie, I am; come in. There's plenty to do as you can see. You've come just in time'.

'Oh I do hope I will be satisfactory. This is my first job and I must set a good example for my younger brothers and sisters'.

'Don't worry Elsie, this is my first job too', said RM. 'I hope we'll both be satisfactory. You look a good strong type, and as you see, Grace Brothers men have given us plenty to do to get all the furniture into place and unpack all these other cases'.

Elsie was satisfactory. She was a tallish, not unattractive, country girl, whose mother had taught her politeness and good manners. She stayed with us about three years until she left to get married. This was about the usual length of stay of housemaids, or even perhaps a little longer than usual. In fact, very soon, by the mid 1950s, housemaids became unprocurable. The post-war social changes provided other, and apparently, more attractive jobs for these girls, especially in the cities. Housemaids in the country lasted a little longer.

Rosemarie worked hard getting the house in order. Making curtains and bedspreads inside the house and organising the garden outside kept her busy. We only had the one car, so her shopping was done on foot to the shops, about half-a-mile away, until we could afford, or rather the bank could afford, another car.

The Austin motor company had just produced another of their successful models—the A/40. My bank manager had faith enough to add another £300 to my already sizable overdraft.

One afternoon, whilst down in our new surgery, RM rang me in tears.

'It won't go round and I can't get it into reverse. It's still out in the street', she stammered out among the tears.

'What won't go round, what do you mean?'

'Now don't get cranky with me, dear. I'll tell you what happened. Stewart Saunders, from Campbell's garage, rang to tell me he was bringing my new car around. He showed me all about it, gave me all the books to do with it and left it at the back door. When he had gone I thought I would take it out the front gate and have a drive. I tried to turn it around to come back in but it won't turn in the street and I can't get it into reverse'.

'Well never mind, I'll come around and see what we can do'.

Our street was the last one in town on the northern end. There were only three other houses in it, with practically no traffic.

There was the shiny new green Austin A/40—'Austin of England' proudly displayed on each side of the bonnet. Sure enough, reverse gear was hard to find. The whole long floor gear lever had to be lifted up and pulled back and to the right. It was stiff and I could understand RM's concern. The other important problem was that Stewart had put long bolts in the front number plate and these projected into the path of the steering rod thus limiting its full movement. Had this not been done, the normal lock would have easily allowed an uninterrupted turn in our street. It had not been long since Sergeant Bedingfield had passed RM for her driving test so she was not full of confidence just then. Later, however, she quickly learnt about country driving and made me proud of her prowess with either car, in any conditions.

* * * * * * * * * *

Paddy Curtin was one of Scone's characters in those days. He had been the carrier for many a year. He had a flat top four-wheel dray, drawn by his faithful Ned. He could be seen all over town delivering goods in all weathers. He was thin as a rake, middle to late age, missing several teeth and much hair, always wearing a thick grey flannel shirt and he usually sat on a pile of sugar bags as his seat. In one street he could be seen delivering a small parcel, in another he could be seen with a piano on his back. The coke for our 'Aga' slow combustion stove was delivered by ten ton lots to the railway yards in bulk. Paddy would bag it and pack it on to his dray, making as many trips as necessary to get it all into one of the horse stables behind the garages, which we set up for coke storage. The whole process might take him all day, yet at the end of three months Paddy's bill would be delivered to the kitchen door, almost with apologies, for the miniscule amount he charged. Everything from library books to furniture and coke, which came to the Scone railway yards for us, would be delivered by Paddy. I can still hear his edentulous drawl—'Good day Doctor, it's a great day'.

Early in 1947, as our new surgery was being completed by the local builder, it was necessary to find a nurse or a sister to join us and live in the flat provided.

Rosemarie and I had been out to dinner to a property, up the Middlebrook, about twelve miles out, and afterwards it was so hot that we all sat around outside on the lawn near the sprinklers. Our hostess, only four weeks ago, had her second child, which came as an unexpected breech presentation, but behaved according to the text books and gave me no worries delivering it. A Karitane nurse was living in the house, a usual custom for about the first 6-8 weeks with a new baby, and she was sitting with us.

'What are you going to do when you finish this job?' I asked Mabs Preston.

'Oh, I think I'll go back to Tasmania. Dad and Mum live in Queenstown and I haven't been back for over a year now. It's much cooler there', she laughed.

Mabs was most pleasant, a brunette, crisp in her speech and her actions, all good traits in a nurse. So I told her about our surgery position and asked her to consider it. She was not greatly interested, so I could only say again, that I would like her to think about it and come in and meet Walter.

A few days later she did. She liked what she saw and I was more than ever impressed.

Mabs Preston agreed to take the job until we could get someone more permanent. She would help out.

She stayed twenty-seven years.

She was not a fully trained nurse. She had done her mothercraft training in which she was certified. This meant she had quite sufficient knowledge of things medical to be in charge of our surgery. The reception, the records and telephone were all cared for by our receptionist. Mabs (we called her our 'Sister') had charge of our examination rooms and the large workroom, where minor procedures were done. She kept her eye on our supplies and was responsible for ordering what was necessary. She was also chief 'tea-maker'—Walter may need three separate tea sessions during an afternoon. Her sleeping and living quarters were very pleasant. We built her a carport. She played bridge and golf and became an active associate member of the new nine-hole golf club, with grass greens, developed by enthusiasts immediately after the war.

She also became a close friend of us both.

* * * * * * * * * *

Vic Hall, who was the first friend I made in Scone in 1940, when I was doing a locum tenens for Walter, had survived the war. He was then in his fifties. Still unmarried, he lived on his property—'Nandowra'—about eight miles out of town where the airstrip had been developed during the war, so that Tiger Moth trainers could land and refuel on their trip to the air training base at Tamworth. He was more interested in this part of his property than the wool-making machines. He was lazy but delightful. There was never need for any prior warning of Vic's visits to our home. Quite frequently, his duties in town done, he would call in and if no one was around he would get comfortable with a book or a car magazine and if it were very hot, as our summers were, he would be found lying on the floor, often sleeping. The floor was always the coolest part of the room. This was long before the days of air-conditioners. Electric fans of various types and sizes were our only relief from the above century days, and often nights. We almost got to an 'air-conditioned' state by placing a block of ice directly in front of the fan. This helped but not as much as we hoped for or expected.

Vic drove an old Marmon saloon, very much a pre-war model, almost completely without upholstery, what paint could be seen was of an old maroon shade, the whole outfit having lost its exhaust system way back in time, so not only could it often be heard approaching with a note like no other car, but it was prone to 'start failures'. Winter starts were almost out of the question so there was always a bed for Vic. Tomorrow would do to start the car! Thank goodness, within a year, his bank manager, in spite of several bad drought years, was compassionate and allowed the purchase of one of the Humber Sixes, as used by staff officers in the war. We were all relieved.

* * * * * * * * * *

Darvall Kater was another frequent visitor to us. He was in his seventies, divorced and had come to live in Scone probably because his brother Charlie had a small property there. They had both come from the western sheep country of New South Wales, near Nyngan where they grew large quantities of wool. Darvall was independent in his habits, and like Vic, needed no invitation. He played at golf and was keen on bridge. He had a small holding on the outskirts of town with a creek and waterholes, which we often sought out on hot weekends. Darvall had many friends, many of whom had gravitated to Scone from the Dubbo area—the 'merino mob'.

* * * * * * * * * *

Scone, at this time and for many years later, had few outside entertainments. The 'Civic' picture theatre would have to be classed as number one. Films were shown six nights a week with two changes of programmes. Perhaps two rodeos a year would be expected in those early post-war years. A picnic race meeting, held over two days, was an annual event at Muswellbrook, fifteen miles away. To this we would often ask city or interstate friends. There were no town baths (the old equivalent of modern swimming centres), no skating rinks, no regular dances but there was a tennis club. This had rather a limited membership completely lacking in talent, except at cake making, and was to be avoided as much as possible.

Improvements were being made within two or more years of the war's end. An RSL club was started and proved popular, except with the doctor. I had a rule never to drink in a hotel because of my profession and my medical upbringing, so this I extended to the RSL club. Anyway it was only active from 5-6 in the evenings, the beer drinking time, and as I rarely finished work till 7 pm it was not part of my orbit. Toby Barton and Walter shared my views.

The Scone Racing Club was developed. An excellent track was established on the river flats and attracted large crowds. There would be a meeting every five or six weeks.

The polo enthusiasts would organise several carnivals with practice matches on Saturdays, so RM and I found some interest here. They were social meeting grounds for those of us not so terribly interested in polo. These opportunities brought people in from all directions, sometimes even 40 or 50 miles away.

There is no doubt the 'pictures' gained our regular custom. Saturday night was pretty regular, Wednesday, if a specially good film was 'on'. We often ridiculed our addiction, making disinterested noises, but ending up by going. The 'doctors' had reserved seats in the third row of the dress circle on the centre aisle. The floor in front of the first seat had a hole about one inch in diameter with a glass insert. Below this was an electric light globe, which, when switched on, would make a flash and so attract the one seated there. The doctors movements were always known. We were never off the phone. One flash of the light meant Walter was needed down on the office phone, two flashes was my call. Sometimes the flash would only mean some phone advice, other times it meant a call away. Theo, the manager, would always know where the doctor had gone so the empty seat could be accounted for as the rest of the party left.

This call system was quite a modern innovation by Theo even though we hated to see the flash. It saved him walking up stairs and disturbing those around by talking. There were, of course, no carpets in picture theatres in those days, even in the dresss circle. Neither was there any heating which meant that in winter, with Scone's freezing temperatures, we went heavily clothed taking a rug and a hot water bag each. The short trip back home in the unheated car meant a dash for a position against the AGA stove, often in competition with neighbours, while the large aluminium kettle boiled for a cup of tea and a filling of the hot water bags to warm the beds. The projection apparatus was quite good as was Theo's selection of films. Some were memorable. Walter Mitty with Danny Kaye's portrayal of his surgeon's role almost put Walter and me into hysterics. On such occasions we would try to keep our foot on the light.

*   *   *   *   *   *   *   *   *   *

'Darling, you are late. We have waited dinner for you'.

'Yes I've been up at 'Brancaster'. I shall probably have to go back. But not for a while'.

In the sitting room Vic and Darvall were comfortably sipping their whisky in front of the large fire. RM who was young and had not started drinking whisky was having her usual dry sherry.

As I was pouring out a glass of lemonade, Elizabeth Foster came up the hall and joined us. She was a locum I had staying with us while Walter was expected to be away for about four weeks. Our practice had grown so much since we established our new surgery and, of course, with time, that to carry on single handed for longer than a few days at a time was far too stressful.

Elizabeth had come in from a call about fifteen miles out. She was a nice gently behaved girl who fitted into the household with ease.

'Why don't you have a whisky?' she asked as she saw me pouring lemonade, 'you are looking tired and after your long day it would do you more good than that lolly water'.

'You're right. It would do me more good, but I will probably have to go back to 'Brancaster' shortly. It looks as though I will have to use the forceps. Mrs Lacey always seems to have large babies. I must tell her to stop'.

'Why not let me go. I have just had six months in residence at Crown Street and have done lots of forceps?'

'Dear Elizabeth, I'm so glad you're here. Thank you for offering. I'm sure you could do it better than I; you've no doubt had much more experience with forceps, which I hate using, but no, I feel I must go when sister rings. Mrs Lacey asked me, only today, to promise to be there for the baby. She knew Walter was away and didn't want the locum. You must understand. It's not that she doesn't want you. It's just that she doesn't know you—that's all. These people are funny. It's not the city, you know'.

'Well, now you're home we'll get on with dinner. Elsie, I know, has everything ready'; so RM led us into the dining room, lemonade and all.

Roast lamb with several vegetables and all the trimmings was always a great meal. While the others had their soup I began carving. The tail had to be kept for Rosemarie, her prerogative, and the fatty gland had to be dissected out from the centre slices, a manoeuvre I had been instructed in, on earlier occasions, by Darvall. In the big sheep country homes, out west, this was always done.

We never drank wines in those days. Although Hunter Valley wines were well known, even in Adelaide, they were not seen in Scone. The vineyards were much lower down the Hunter towards Newcastle. Also wine drinking with meals in post-war Australia had not really started, certainly not in Scone.

'What brought you to town today?' I asked Vic.

'I came to sell ten bulls' pizzles' was his answer.

'Well that's an odd way to put it. I suppose you mean you have sold ten bulls at the sale. Not a very nice way to talk in front of young Elizabeth', said Darvall.

'I'm the youngest here' objected Rosemarie 'what about that?'

'You're married and Elizabeth isn't' put in Darvall.

'Well', said Vic, 'it was perhaps an odd way of putting it, and I'm sorry I did Rosemarie, please forgive me. The sale was so good, like your whisky, that my manners slipped'.

'That's all right Vic, you're forgiven'.

'Forgiven for what. What is a bull's pizzle anyway?' spoke up Elizabeth, 'I've never heard of the word'.

Lots of silence all round the table, everyone looking at everyone else until Elizabeth's cheeks got very red. She blushed easily. She began to realise what a bull's pizzle was.

Sale days were normally on Fridays so town was crowded that day. An extra day would occasionally be used for a 'special lot' sale. Good business was expected by the retailers and all the business people as well as those organising the street stalls for various charities. The doctors saw little of these goings on. Friday was just another day, the lists of appointments a bit longer than usual. Our surgery helpers always stayed till the last patient was shown in.

There were nearly always one or more house calls or a hospital visit to be done before going home. Dinner on sale days was rarely before eight

What's a bulls pizzle anyway!

48

and the number of diners was in doubt. RM would tell me of a frequent happening—a voice at the door . . .

'Anyone home—what's for dinner?'

If, for her own reason, she wished no more diners, she would answer . . .

'Cottage pie tonight'.

'Oh goodbye, I'll see what's on at the Hallidays'.

Lamb in all its forms was much more used than beef. The butchers were excellent but much was the wrath they received if mutton were delivered.

CHAPTER NINE

A Fundamental Lesson . . .
For Young Doctors

Breakfast on a Tuesday was always at seven. Elsie was punctual. The hot plate had a dish with fried eggs, sausages and some bacon. Toast was at the ready alongside the coffee percolator.

'What have you got on this morning, anything exciting?', RM would often ask as we helped ourselves.

'Yes, we don't get many gall-bladders to do, but Walter has a rather fat man who has gall-stones as well as a history of many inflammatory attacks, so he should be difficult, which really means exciting. I'll give him his anaesthetic and when I have him settled down to a nice state of relaxation I shall put him on the ether machine and assist Walt.'

'How do you manage to keep him controlled when you are scrubbed up and assisting at the operation?''

'"Just talent!! No, really, it's pretty simple; the little ether pump has a tap control so that if his breathing should alter its rhythm I just ask the theatre nurse to make an alteration to a tap. We use this method for all our major ops. when we assist each other. Its quite safe and very simple. The slightest change in the breathing you can detect immediately, it's a subconscious as well as a conscious observation. What are you doing today?'

'I'm picking up Betty Halliday around ten o'clock and we are going up to the Latham's at Ellerston for lunch. Nellie has been asking us for some time and today suits. Can I have the Vauxhall instead of my Austin?'

'Why, is there something 'off' with the A/40?'

'No, no, she's all right, you won't have any trouble with it. But you know there has been a fair bit of rain lately and they probably had more up in the hills there yesterday than we had here. You've always told me how quickly some of those creeks can rise and I figure the Vauxhall is a bit higher and has two more cylinders anyway, so we should be safer— don't you think?'

'Sure, you take it. But if the creeks are up you'd better listen to Betty. She knows more about creeks than you do. Just be careful.'

'What was that ring you had just before breakfast?''

'It was from a Mrs Stapleton at Muswellbrook. She asked could she see me this morning and I had to explain that it was our operating morning but I should be back at the surgery by twelve. That, she said, would suit her. We don't get many patients up from Muswellbrook. Yank has a pretty strong grip on things. There are always a few, though, who want to see someone else. It tends to flatter me a bit, but I suppose that's silly. Perhaps the younger doctor subconsciously seeks an 'ego' boost'. I must be off now—be careful', as I kissed RM and dashed off.

* * * * * * * * * *

'I thought this chap would worry me. He's not only so fat but all these wretched adhesions from his previous attacks make it a risky operation. They tend to make it much harder to find the common bile duct. It often gets pulled out of place by the adhesions,' Walter was muttering away as he delved deep and I kept the field dry.

'You know up there in our POW hospital in Batavia I assisted a Dutch surgeon do two gall-bladders and his method was different. He told me they were taught to do the operation in a reverse way. They start at the fundus and work down to the cystic duct, while the British method goes for the duct first and then works the gall-bladder out backwards. Wouldn't it be easier in this case to do it the Dutch way?'

'Well my surgical tutors in Edinburgh taught me to get the cystic artery and duct first. Maybe the Dutch method would be easier, but look, isn't that the common bile duct there?' Walter was a good surgeon and very pleasant to work with. He got through his problem and we had a cup of tea in the surgeons' room where we found Toby Barton having his. There were two minor ops. yet to be done.

'What mischief are you chaps getting into?' asked our senior colleague, 'did you cut his common bile duct? If you did he'll be yellow in a week.'

Toby was always on for a little dig with that friendly twinkle in his eyes, just screwed up a little bit. We all got on very well.

Mrs Stapleton was waiting for me in the surgery when I got there a bit late.

'This is a very nice place you have here. Much better than the Muswellbrook surgery'.

She was well dressed in a tweed suit over a yellow blouse and a scarf. I noticed a gold brooch on the left lapel and small gold earrings. I guessed her age at around forty. She seemed relaxed and confident with an easy smile. I wondered why she had come to me.

Her periods were the trouble as she described them to me as 'being all over the place'.

'It makes life so difficult and uncertain. Only last week I was out to lunch at Denman when I began to have a flooding. You know doctor, that can be most embarrassing'.

She told me how she had lost her husband two years ago in a boating accident off the Queensland coast, where she used to live. The reason she came to live in Muswellbrook was because her sister and her husband had a large property out on the Denman road. She had bought a small cottage in town and had made quite a lot of friends. She had no children. She played golf and bridge and was happy apart from these 'periods'. She had no pain or other complaints. However she said, 'I know I have a fibroid because several doctors have told me so'.

She had kept her figure and her abdomen was not covered in fat, as was so in many women of her age. I could feel an enlarged uterus which I confirmed on vaginal examination. I thought it felt a bit soft, but then I thought this could have been due to some degeneration in the fibroid. It could have been a pregnant uterus from its soft feel. But then she was a widow and she told me how other doctors had noticed this enlarged uterus, so I really didn't think it was a pregnant uterus. However it would be wise to get a urine test done to exclude a pregnancy.

I did not tell her my thoughts. I agreed with her and her other doctors that her uterus was enlarged but otherwise I could find no abnormality. I pointed out that with all my new patients on their first visit I liked to have a urine test, just as I checked their blood pressure and did other routines.

'I thought you would want to do that doctor so I brought up a sample of urine I passed just before leaving home' as she produced a nice clean bottle from her bag with her name on it.

We discussed her problem and her good health generally and I went on to explain that we were beginning to understand the causes of these period irregularities much better in the last two years. There were many new female hormone preparations available to treat such problems.

'That's why I came to you doctor. I have heard from several people that you have taken a particular interest in women's problems, and that you are getting quite a name'.

'Well, thank you. I am particularly interested and spend a bit of time in the women's hospitals in Sydney whenever I am down'.

So I gave her some treatment and her urine to sister.

'Are you sure this injection you gave me and these pills will stop any further flooding?'

'I am hopeful, never sure. But wait a week or two and then see me again'.

'If they don't help doctor can I have a hysterectomy?'

'Let's wait and see', as I showed her to the door.

I was anxious to get out to sister to make sure she didn't just test the urine and throw the rest away. I wanted to have a pregnancy test done and needed it.

'I thought you might need it doctor, so I kept it'.

The urine had to be sent to the laboratory in Newcastle where it would be injected into frogs which gave a quicker result than the older type test using mice. I could get the result in four days.

The report of the test came back 'negative' for pregnancy in the mail

52

on the next Monday. So did Mrs Stapleton, who had a late appointment in the afternoon's consult.

She was shown in, looking anxious this time and a bit paler, saying she had not got any relief from my treatment. Would I do a hysterectomy, was her question. She had heard how well my patients did after this operation.

I cogitated. The pregnancy test was negative, she had this fibroid that other doctors had found and she was still complaining. I examined her again, and neither now nor earlier had I seen blood. The uterus was still enlarged and a bit tender. I could see no reason for not suggesting a hysterectomy. Whether I could control her symptoms with larger doses of hormone or even with different hormones, would take time to discover. She wanted a hysterectomy. Why not!! I liked doing the operation.

We were late leaving the surgery that night and Walt and I met as we discussed tomorrow's operating list.

'By the way, did I see Mrs Stapleton from Muswellbrook leaving the surgery this afternoon?' he asked.

'Yes, that's the second time she has come to see me. She was here last week. I have put her down for a hysterectomy next Tuesday'.

'Have you done a pregnancy test?'

'Yes, here's the report, it came this morning'.

Walter grunted as he walked back to his room with some papers. He had a duodenal ulcer which was always a source of chronic pain to him and a worry to me. He often got a bit 'testy' especially on long afternoon consults. That's why he was always drinking cups of tea and taking alkaline stomach tablets.

When I opened Mrs Stapleton's abdomen and packed off the intestines as Walter lowered the head of the table, which position was necessary for this type of pelvic operation, I saw her uterus was larger than normal and both ovaries looked quite healthy. As she was only 40 I decided to leave them both and got on with the operation I had planned—a total hysterectomy.

'Do you want a hand there?'

'No thanks Walt, sister and I can do this. It should be a piece of cake with no adhesions to worry about and nice relaxation from your end'.

'Everyone's happy then', mumbled Walter.

When we were having our cup of tea he asked me if I had opened the uterus. Just then sister came in with the uterus in a glass jar saying, 'You'll probably want to send this away to Newcastle for pathology'.

'Yes, thanks sister'.

'I don't bet as you know, but I'm sure you'll find more than a fibroid when you open it', was Walter's comment.

Sure enough—a little Joey!

Walter then went on to tell me a bit about my new patient. Not much gossip of Scone or the district failed to pass through his sieve. She was an attractive widow of Muswellbrook. Eighteen months earlier, before I had rejoined the practice, she paid Walter a visit with the same story. He picked her and gave her an unco-operative 'cold shoulder' which she recognised and wasted no further time. Walter's spies found out that she visited Newcastle for a short stay in a small private hospital.

'I had my doubts about her. But then her urine test came back negative, which made me doubt my doubts'.

'OK, but whose urine was it?' grinned Walter.

'Sure, I agree, I have lots to learn, especially about women. Her approach was new to me, and anyway I am quite out of touch with women. In fact it would be truer to say I've never been in touch with women—not that sort anyway. I shall remember her and how she 'conned' me. But don't forget I've made her happy. I have cured her complaints, I enjoyed the surgery and she will probably remain a patient of ours, that's good medicine, isn't it?'

'If seeing the foetus doesn't worry you'.

'No, I can't say that upsets me. It certainly doesn't upset Mrs Stapleton, for I'm sure she knew she was pregnant. I think she has been clever for she got what she wanted. If you think about it, from her point of view, she was caught in the pregnancy trap. She didn't want it, she probably never wanted a child, she was not that sort of woman. She obviously didn't want her uterus, at forty it was an absolute liability. I think it must be for most women at that age. If they've wanted kids they've probably had them by then. The risk of a mongol is not worth facing then anyway'.

'I can see the arguments. It's probably a little harder for me than it is for you, Les, to be undisturbed when a pregnancy is jettisoned for no sound medical reason. I'm older than you and probably have been influenced more heavily by Victorian ideas. Also you have seen so much more, in the last few years, of the needless loss of life. Your feelings are no doubt more liberal than mine. Perhaps I shall change—in time'.

'Well in Mrs Stapleton's case I haven't got the slightest feeling of any guilt. As I've said those involved are all happy'.

'What about the foetus?'

'Now, come on Walt; you don't think really that it could be happy or unhappy. If it had gone on to become an unwanted child with no legitimate father, it would have reason to be unhappy. I think, as time goes by, there will be a much more liberal approach to the whole question of unwanted pregnancies. No doubt there will be strong emotions and much argument but in the end, don't you think, it is the woman's right to decide whether she wants to give birth to, and bring up, a child. Shouldn't she make the decision?'

'If we don't have lunch soon we'll be doing our afternoon surgery on empty stomachs and mine hurts', as Walter ended the discussion.

* * * * * * * * * *

Sep was there in front of the fire when I got home that evening.

'Where are the girls. Aren't they home yet? I've forgotten where they were supposed to be going today. Oh, I remember, out to Bunnan, wasn't it?'

'Nope to the first—yep to the second. I saw your car had left the surgery so I reckoned you'd be looking for someone to help you drink a whisky. It's probably been raining some more but if they were in any trouble we should have heard'.

'Yes RM has had her licence for only a year but she can handle these country roads and creeks pretty well. One day recently she found out for herself that to get out of Omadale Brook, when it was sticky on the approach, she could only do it in reverse. That's pretty good, don't you think?'

'You should put some of those new Olympic tyres on the rear wheels. They've got a new tread designed for creeks and slippery grades'.

'Yea, I'll look into it. Any murders around the district today?'

'Are you just guessing or did you hear about it?'

'Of course I was guessing. Why, has there really been a murder?'

'I don't know', said Sep. 'I can't really say anything at present, even if I couldn't hear the girls coming up the hall right now'.

'Well, you're late. Have a good trip?' as RM put up her lips.

'Full of excitement, both there and getting there. The creeks were up and there was some shooting at lunch time. I think someone was shot. Have you heard anything Sep?' as Betty moved over to kiss him.

'I've had a ring from the Bunnan police station, but 'mum's' the word,' as he smiled that smirky smile, which I called his 'solicitor's smile'.

The girls joined us, Betty with a whisky, RM with her usual dry sherry. Our cocker spaniel, 'Shadow', was always so pleased when we got together round the fireplace. He loved to have his family all in one piece. He went and sat at RM's feet.

We were given all the Bunnan gossip and heard about their great new engine for electricity generation. The phone rang just as Elsie came in to ask RM about some dinner arrangements. It was a call from Sergeant Bedingfield to tell me an ambulance was bringing in a man who had been shot at Bunnan. Would I see him at the hospital after he was admitted?

'You'll know more about the shooting at Bunnan than I do', commented Sep, as he and Betty were leaving. They would not accept RM's invitation to stay for dinner. Betty wanted to get home for some calls she was expecting and she was tired after the day's affairs.

The victim had a couple of through and through bullet wounds in his thigh, he would not die. A tetanus injection and some dressings were all that was required, before he was handed over to the Sergeant for questioning.

I did enjoy country practice.

CHAPTER TEN

A Cure For Infertility

Once I settled down to my general practice routine and had every Wednesday afternoon devoted to pregnancy cases, I found I became extremely interested in this aspect of medical practice. It began to dawn on me that my future years in medicine would probably centre around midwifery, or, to use the more modern term, obstetrics. My war years had been overburdened with the care of males, so maybe these feelings which were developing for the care of, and the problems of, pregnant women were nature's attempt to balance my clincial experiences, by correcting a sort of medical malnutrition (a term we lived with as prisoners of war) or was it simply that I admired women more than men? Whatever it was, I enjoyed and looked forward to my Wednesday afternoon clinics. Because I enjoyed it, I think I did it well. I found most of my medical reading was to do with women, their pregnancies and their problems. Whenever I got a chance to attend post-graduate sessions in Sydney, I found myself either at the Royal Hospital for Women or at King George V Hospital.

Much progress had been made in the handling of obstetric problems and many new diseases were to be studied since my student training days, before the war. The problems of the Rhesus factor were unfolding, the control of puerperal infections, the increased safety in all the operative aspects of obstetrics and especially pain relief in childbirth, all stimulated my interest. The investigation of infertility was of particular interest to me because of one particular young lady, who had married into one of the biggest pastoral families of this great country district.

Shall we call her Roberta, for ethical reasons, and also because I knew of no one of that name? Roberta's engagement to the only son of this leading family was hailed with much enthusiasm by both families for she came from one of the important business families of Sydney. The wedding was lavish and hailed by the social columnists of the day as the cream of their year's assignments.

The family histories on both sides were given to the waiting readers of the daily newspapers and the best magazines and no one could find any skeletons, or even 'any just cause' why this should not be a most satisfactory union. I was the first to find a problem.

The wedding took place in 1944 when her husband had been discharged after distinguished service in the Middle East and later in New Guinea. He had been awarded the much coveted blue and white ribbon and a nasty fracture of his left forearm which caused the surgeons much trouble, who then judged it sufficient cause for his discharge from the army.

One Wednesday afternoon, somewhere in mid 1947 Roberta came to see me. She was worried that she had not got pregnant even though they had both hoped for such an event.

I had met her socially some months earlier. A most attractive medium type blond, widely set blue eyes, slightly taller than average, with what seemed to me a beautiful figure, and an easy smile, all made for a desirable person to know and be with. She was twenty-six years old and thought it high time she should join my Wednesday afternoon queue.

Her story revealed a pleasant upbringing, with average results at school although the war had interfered with the planned European finish. She had represented her school at swimming and lawn tennis and had been popular. She would have missed out on many of the normal teenage social affairs, because of the war, but with her attractions she would not have lacked male escorts. I would have judged her to have gone to the altar as a V.I.

She had no history of notable illnesses in her past, except a heavy dose of Rubella in 1941, when it swept Australia. This was, of course, good news, for rubella if contracted in the early weeks of pregnancy could cause havoc with the foetal senses.

Her husband, whom we shall call Jim, seemed a pretty healthy country type, who had no unusual health problems in his past. He was the eldest of three children of this pastoral family, there being two sisters, both married. Roberta told me their marriage was happy, especially in bed, and that, as a city girl, she had adapted to country life like a fish to water.

She looked to me a perfectly healthy female, whose hormones, no normal male would question. However, I was obliged to examine her and found no evidence of any abnormalities wherever I looked. My sister had tested her urine, which she had brought with her, and I took a sample of blood, which I would send away for various tests. I took a chest x-ray for she told me this had never been done.

There are many reasons why these obviously healthy looking couples seem to have difficulty establishing a pregnancy. I always believed that one should push the optimistic button and in general talk about 'nature taking her time'. 'When she is ready, you'll get pregnant' and so on.

Roberta quickly quipped back, that she was ready and didn't care about waiting for nature.

'What will you do now?' was her question.

There are three basic elements for establishing a pregnancy. The male must be capable of depositing a load of healthy sperms at the neck of the womb, at the right time of the month. The woman must be ovulating and her Fallopian tubes must be open and capable of transporting the egg or eggs from her ovary to the cavity of the womb. From that point on the sperm and the egg can get together and know what to do.

I had already learnt that to ask for the husband to come in and see me, too early in the piece, was inclined to upset him. The ones I had experience with were usually hard working farmers who did not appreciate any questions about their virility. So, I had thus already developed my own methods. The women, much more sensible creatures, never minded questions directed to whether they were ovulating and whether they had menstrual problems.

A woman who menstruates regularly, is usually ovulating, but it is essential, and usually pretty easy, to confirm this. Immediately before the developing egg bursts out from the ovary, the body temperature, which is extraordinarily constant in all weathers, rises about 1° Fahrenheit. The time of the egg's release is always constant, about fourteen days before the next period is due. So that, if the woman is having regular periods at about twenty-eight day intervals, she ovulates about mid-cycle.

It is quite simple to get women to agree to take their mouth temperature on first waking in the morning, especially over these few days in the middle of the month, or better still, every morning so that they can appreciate the pattern of the mid-cycle rise. I had special temperature charts which I gave these women and explained how I wanted them to record each morning's temperature, before the cup of tea, and before getting out of bed.

This was always a good start to the investigations and usually accepted without complaint. Roberta would do this. She had heard about others who had done it. She would see me after three months recording. Meanwhile there was nothing else to do except lead a normal life.

If, in three months, the chart showed this mid-cycle rise in temperature, it would prove she was ovulating normally and I would then have to check that her tubes were patent. Sometimes at the moment of ovulaton, some women experience a lower abdominal pain, in the midline, just like a 'windy' pain, which may last for a few hours, not a bad pain, more in the nature of discomfort. It was always worth mentioning this, for some good observers could make use of this knowledge.

Now, to test whether the Fallopian tubes are open or closed most specialists would seek x-ray help. At the right time of the month, they would inject an opaque dye up into the uterus, under pressure, and check, with the x-ray, whether it passed out one or other tube. This is positive evidence.

I was able to use another type of test, called Rubin's test, after the man who first reported it, but I made my own modification. It was easy to make a little set consisting of a soda water sparklet bulb (carbon dioxide gas) hooked into line with the blood pressure machine and a special nozzle with an air tight fit into the neck of the womb. As the carbon dioxide gas was released, gently, the pressure in the womb would rise, and be recorded on the blood pressure machine, until it reached 110 or 120 mm mercury. Then, if one or other tube were open, the gas would escape out into the general abdominal cavity and the pressure would drop to 70 or 80 mm. This showed me one or both tubes were open, In fact, as I got more clever, I could pick which tube was letting the gas out. That didn't matter however. Another point to confirm this was, as the woman got up from the couch and stood up, she would usually say 'ouch', and then tell me she had a pain in her shoulder. This was expected and showed that the gas had risen to irritate the diaphragm. Sometimes, if in any doubt with my gas test I would inject dye and take an x-ray. The gas test had the obvious advantages of cost and no radiation.

Roberta came back with her chart. She could notice the mid-cycle rise in the temperature. She was looking great and said, 'Hooray, hooray, I'm ovulating'. Country practice was much more earthy than city practice.

'Now' she said 'what do we do next?'

'I'll have to test your tubes, and this has to be done just after your period clears up'.

'Well, I'm just expecting one shortly, so can we do the test after that?'

'Yes, that's OK', and I explained to her what I would do.

Both her tubes were open. I could find no reason in her why she could not get pregnant so it was time to think of Jim. He would be conditioned by now to expect this. I explained how I wanted a sample of his semen and told them to have intercourse and for him to withdraw and make his emission into a clean jar, wrap it in cottonwool, keep it warm and bring it in as soon as possible. It had to be kept warm otherwise the sperms would lose their motility.

Roberta rang me when this was about to happen so I was waiting in the surgery that morning as she came hurrying in with a smile from ear to ear.

'Oh dear, did we have fun', as she dived into her large handbag and pulled out a hot water bottle. 'We didn't want it to get cold so we did it, with the hot water bottle alongside us, and as soon as Jim put it in the jar I screwed the cap on and put it inside the hot water bottle cover. It's been alongside me on the car seat all the way in. Hope I haven't boiled it'.

It is a very simple examination. The amount of emission is easily measured when a drop is put on a slide and examined under the microscope. A healthy sample shows myriads of sperms, which look like little tadpoles, wriggling madly in all directions. This proves they are healthily active, as well as being able to see that most are quite normal in size and shape. Some few are usually abnormal, having no tails or abnormal shaped heads, but these would never get into the egg before a healthy one, so they don't matter.

Jim's test was normal. Now came the crunch; what would I do next?

I explained to Roberta that the timing of intercourse was most important. The egg, when it leaves the ovary, is normally very quickly picked up by the end of the Fallopian tube and carried along to meet the sperms which have wriggled up through the womb. If the timing of this meeting is delayed, one or other will die, usually within twenty-four hours. So I impressed on her why it was important to have intercourse just after ovulation, and not to keep the egg waiting too long.

'I don't think you could accuse us of that' she laughed, as she told me there were few days that slipped by without this chance of such an introduction.

Anyway, I again stressed the importance of the timing and asked her to continue to keep her temperature and whenever it showed that all important rise she was to seek out her husband and request a 'service.'

Some weeks went by when Roberta came in again, rather depressed, which was unusual. She and Jim had been queried by the parents as to when they were going to give them a grandchild, which made them feel a little guilty; even beginning to regard themselves as actors do, when the reviews are bad.

She never remained depressed for long. She began to laugh as she went on to tell me how one day, only a couple of weeks back, she was alone, getting some lunch, as Jim would not be back till nightfall. She thought she would take her temperature, it must have been nearly time for ovulation. To her surprise it was a degree and a half higher than it was that morning. She had not had any cup of tea so she thought of Jim. They were in the middle of shearing. She saddled her horse and galloped away to the shed, rushed in among all the hands and got Jim. They rushed back, and in an atmosphere of greasy wool skirtings, had intercourse. Perhaps this would be lucky. They really were trying all that I had told them. It was two weeks later, during her next menses, that she was with me now.

We had a long talk. I knew that this feeling of guilt would not help them. In fact it was well known that the longer the delay in achieving a conception, the less the likelihood of success. So often at this stage, or later, the despairing couple would consider an adoption.

This, they had thought of and discussed but were not too keen. I pointed out that it would not be difficult to obtain a well chosen baby from Sydney, where I had several specialist friends and I also knew Matron Shaw, of the Crown Street Women's Hospital. I had also heard of several cases in which soon after an adoption the couples achieved natural conception. Roberta and I discussed many aspects until I got the feeling that Jim thought it time to take their problem to the world of the Sydney specialists. His father, and Roberta's father were both members of an old established club in Sydney and had obviously talked about the children's problem and were making various suggestions.

In a way, I was sorry that I had not been able to play a more successful role than to do the various tests I had done. I knew of no treatment, so maybe, I should positively suggest a referral to a Macquarie Street specialist.

Armed with a long letter, which outlined the tests I had done and the findings, Roberta and Jim drove off to Sydney.

My specialist colleague answered my letter and outlined his approach, which included some hospital investigations such as a curettage and x-rays. Also, because Jim had been to New Guinea, a leading physician was to be consulted to exclude any rare tropical blood disorders. Everything that Macquarie Street could offer, even unto several consultations with a psychiatrist, who seemed to specialise in this problem, would be done.

I was surprised, a few weeks later, to receive, in the morning's mail, a long letter from a Macqaurie Street psychiatrist. It told of a course of hypnosis that Roberta had undergone, somewhat querulously, in which a problem she had when at school with one of the prefects, who objected to the way she did her hair, had surfaced. Roberta had refused to make the necessary changes ordered by the prefect and the psychiatrist was beginning to build on this. What utter balderdash. My opinion of psychiatrists, who tried to 'con' me on my return from prisoner-of-war life, was well known. Being a clinician, who by now in my career, had gathered a few clues about some aspects of the medical profession and its devious ways, I was learning to be very suspicious of who I called the 'trick cyclists'. They were certainly in their 'running–in' period; which I doubted they would ever leave. Poor Roberta, what a load of rubbish.

Jim's experiences were not much better. He was being given the run-around too. The psychiatrists didn't get him, but the pathologists did. They wanted to look at his testicular cells. On the advice of his physician he was sent to a urologist to have a testicular biopsy taken. I knew his sperms were normal. I had seen them in action. Not good enough. The pathologist wanted to see the cells they came from—the testicular biopsy was therefore essential.

Jim was admitted to hospital and prepared for an anaesthetic. Testicular biopsies were relatively new, even being discussed in women's magazines. In due course a piece of his testicle was put under the microscope. Instead of leaving hospital in 24 hours, as he had been promised, he was kept there two weeks. The biopsy led to a haemorrhage with a large blood clot. Within twenty-four hours this was infected. An abscess with much pain developed. This had to be drained requiring a long stay in hospital.

Roberta was horrified; what had they done to her Jim? She visited him daily, wondering why on earth they had let themselves get into this situation. She had been brainwashed. Had he been ruined?

'For God's sake, let us get home' she implored, 'before they can think up anything else. Les would never get us into this mess. I want to go back to talk to him.'

*　*　*　*　*　*　*　*　*

What a 'to do' that was. I've never had a worse time in my life. I suppose Jim, in his war years, may have had worse, but all this in Sydney was so self inflicted. I'd never agree to anything like that again.

Roberta's sense of humour was returning, for all this. She said it in a way that past horrors should be dealt with.

'Yes, I heard about most of your problems. I suppose I must take the blame for sending you off to Sydney to the ''so-called'' experts.

'Oh, no, no', Jim hastened to add, 'we didn't mean to be critical of you, I am sure Robby would agree. You only did what we wanted, for I'm sure you knew our parents were anxious for us to get other opinions. No, please don't think we were being critical of you, quite the reverse. In fact, several times Robby and I talked about you, while we were being tortured in Sydney and wished you were there. Those chaps down in Macquarie Street may have higher degrees, but God, could they do with your manner!! We were kept waiting, we often got the impression that we should be grateful to them for deigning to see us, they told us little about what was being done and the results. Did you hear about their last effort? I'd like to show you, can we go into the examination room?'

He pulled down his trousers and showed me a distorted, enlarged, bruised and rather horrible looking scrotum, quite red, with a gauze pad stuck to it, for it was still discharging.

'It's so damned sore. I couldn't sit properly to drive the car up from Sydney. Robby had to drive. Do you think it will ever be any good again?'

My job always was to comfort, so I assured him it would settle down and he and his Robby would again be happy in bed.

'When Les, how long do you reckon?'

'Oh, it shouldn't be long for that discharge to stop, and this area always heals quickly. I'd say another week would make all the difference. Come and see me then'.

Roberta gave me her story of the hypnosis sessions. It was all rather sickening to me, and, I would guess, quite unnecessary.

'What will we do now?; Roberta asked.

'Well, I guess you should get out home and feel lucky that you are safely back after—how long was it Roberta?'

'We were away from home for nearly six weeks, all rotten and I think best forgotten. We are not going to have any more investigation or anything else in Macquarie Street. If you can't get us pregnant we'll not bother any further'.

'I think we should look on the bright side of all this. You never know, going through all those traumas that you both did, it is possible that something that we don't understand has changed, and you may find a surprise happens. In the meanwhile I think your attitude to this apparent infertility has changed for the better. It seems to me you'll not care about it so much as you were doing before you went to Sydney. Take my advice and forget about it all now and get back to the property and on with your work'.

I wondered if I should offer them some Valium, but they both assured me they would prefer not to take any pills.

'If I don't see you before, come and let's have another talk in about six months', and off they went.

I honestly didn't know what more I could do for them at present. It was no good giving them Vitamin E tablets, which were all the rage and the 'in' thing in the medical journals for unexplained infertility. It was supposed to be a stimulant to fertility, but personally I would have thought drinking a glass of water under a Rowan tree, as recommended by the Scottish highlanders, would be equally as effective. The Scots probably did a little more under the Rowan tree than the legend relates.

Anyway, I thought if I gave them anything they might start hoping because of it, and I wanted them to forget the whole business for a while.

I had not given them much thought for some months when Roberta came in, unannounced, one morning just as I came into the surgery from my hospital rounds.

'Guess what', she giggled.

'Don't tell me the stork is on his way?'

'Highly likely' Roberta pronounced, as she threw her head back, saying, 'I've missed two periods and I feel a bit "squiffy" in the mornings. You'd better check it for me'.

Sure enough, she was pregnant.

'There', I said, feeling a little smug, 'you see, didn't I tell you to go home and forget all about it and a surprise might happen', when she pulled me up with a start.

'It's no thanks to you or to all those clever friends of yours down in Sydney. So much for all the specialists. I'll tell you something that you should remember when next you have a problem like ours'.

She went on to tell me about a friend of hers from Queensland whom she knew was also trying to have a baby. She hadn't seen her for quite a while until they met at a polo carnival in Armidale some months back. There was her friend, surrounded with her husband's polo ponies and in the back of the station wagon Roberta saw a bassinet with a little baby in it.

'Is that yours, Susie?' she excitedly asked. When Susie beamed that it was, Roberta was so excited for her and hugged and kissed her.

'How on earth did you manage it, after all those years of trying?'

'Well', said Susie, 'It's so easy. None of those specialists I went to in Brisbane helped us one jot. Granny did it!!'

'What do you mean, "Granny did it"?' asked Roberta.

'Well, you know how old fashioned Grannies are, we had never mentioned the subject of our difficulty having a baby to her, for this sort of conversation was not openly discussed "in her day". However she was visiting us some months back, when my mother was also with us, and she told Granny that we had tried to have a baby, but couldn't. When she heard this she said 'What nonsense, why didn't you tell me before? I know what to do and could have told you years ago, if only you had asked'. So I asked Granny for the recipe. "Stand on your head" she pronounced'.

'When I recovered from this, I, rather flippantly, asked, 'before—after—or during'?'

'Don't be so daft dear, you work that out for yourselves. In my day it never failed'.

'So', said Susie, 'we did what she said. You can imagine the bedroom gymnastics'.We split our sides laughing.

'Anyway, it worked and there in the truck is the result'.

Roberta could hardly wait to tell Jim. They tried Granny's treatment.

'You probably don't believe it's got anything to do with it, but I am now pregnant. You have assured me that's so'.

When I recovered I thanked Roberta for the lesson which I would not only remember, but would dine out on for many a dinner.
'JUST STAND ON YOUR HEAD'

CHAPTER ELEVEN

'The mind is its own place, and in it self
Can make a Heav'n of Hell, a Hell of Heav'n.'

John Milton, Paradise Lost Bk. 1

There are other causes of infertility, except those which are purely medical. Some are explained on purely psychological grounds, while others are simply put down to the 'whim' of Nature. I encountered one cause, an extremely difficult one to manage, which could be put down to the 'whim' (not womb!) of woman.

This was the lot of a grazing family from the Muswellbrook district. The only son of this large property met and fell in love with a young lady, the elder daughter of a family living in the Scone district.

Ethel, shall we call her, came back after her boarding school days in Sydney to live with her parents on the property. She was a vivacious tall brunette with attractive green eyes, set in with a 'smutty finger' and long hair which she dressed in different fashions for different occasions. She had always loved horses, since her first pony, and had naturally taken to the study of horse-blood lines. If the many studs around Scone had not sparked her interest in this subject they were certainly her major hobby, now that she had left school. The stud book was well thumbed. There was rarely a stallion or a mare whose pedigree she did not know. Horses and horse racing could therefore be considered as her absorbing interest.

Ethel met this only son of the Muswellbrook property, shall we call him Sandy, at a picnic race meeting in Muswellbrook in 1947. Sandy was twenty-three, nearly four years older than Ethel. His father had developed their seven thousand acre holding in the hilly country to the east of the town. Misfortune resulting from a tractor accident severely restricted his father's movements just at the time Sandy was finishing his Leaving Certificate year at Kings School in 1944. He had made up his mind to go on to Law School but had to reconsider this after his father's accident. He debated his future for a month in the new year of 1945, before he decided to take over the management of the property, for a year at least, to see how that life would suit him. He considered he could return to his legal leanings should his skills on property management not develop.

As the year progressed Sandy found himself happy with his decision. He got on well with the other workers on the place, and fitted in well at home after his six years away at boarding school. The war came to an end that year bringing an increased interest in primary production. He could see his future now before him.

He spent many evenings talking over the future of the place with his father. It had been primarily a cattle breeding property but now they planned to buy in a neighbouring property and concentrate on sheep as well as cattle. This was all very exciting and was Sandy's every thought until that day at the picnic races in 1947.

Ethel was in well cut riding clothes with an emerald green blouse; her hair worn long and free. They had not met before. It was in the marquee, as their parents were having afternoon tea together, that they were introduced. His good looks and her attractions, in the setting of a picnic race meeting, had obvious consequences. Sandy now had something else to think about.

The romance blossomed. The parents were equally happy as the young couple visited each others property and discussed future plans. Wedding invitations were sent out for the tenth of April 1948, Ethel's twentieth birthday.

Ethel's parents had been patients of Walter's since his arrival in 1932. He had been to their property many times both professionally and with Gwen on social occasions. RM and I had also been invited to the wedding ceremony, in the local village church and afterwards to the homestead reception, as were 150 others. The uniting of two respected families in the country always makes for an extremely happy and mutually congratulatory occasion. This was no exception.

I had got to know Sandy a bit as a result of a minor accident he had during his courting days. He suffered rather a nasty cut on his left arm just above the elbow. Ethel brought him into the surgery one Wednesday afternoon when Walter was off duty and I was conducting my obstetrical clinic. Mabs got everything ready and we put a few stitches in the wound and gave him a tetanus injection. I saw him through that affair and had met him once or twice more before the wedding. We got on well and liked one another. He was excited with his bride-to-be, which was great to watch. They were a fortunate pair. Both were born into most comfortable situations while Sandy's education and age allowed him to escape the war. The future looked good.

Rosemarie was not much older than Ethel; liked her and they often got together for a chat on equestrian occasions. Polo and polo practices became fairly regular events on Saturdays, in the winter, so we saw quite a bit of both Ethel and Sandy. They told us of the new home they were building and wanted us to see it when it was finished.

RM who was an acute observer, mentioned on our way home one Saturday evening, that she wondered how Ethel and Sandy were getting on.

'What do you mean? They're happy enough, aren't they?'

'I just wondered. Ethel sat in the car and talked to me a lot today. She didn't say anything definite but I just got an impression that there may be a problem; probably my hyper acute and unreliable intuition.'

Several months later Ethel's mother, an old friend of Walter's, began coming to see him every time she was in town. I noticed her frequent visits but gave it no thought. After one of these visits Walter did mention to me that they were hoping Ethel would get on and have a baby, they were anxious for grandchildren. He listened, as he always did, with a sympathetic ear, but admitted he knew nothing of the young couple's plans. I wasn't interested in their plans either.

Not until one day, several weeks later. Sandy saw me at the post office, collecting the mail.

'Hullo doctor, fancy your getting the mail, I thought the girls did that.'

'Hi Sandy; yes, just a slave to the surgery, but I like it. What are you doing out of your territory, and at this early hour?'

'I needed a portion of a hydraulic line for the tractor and Campbells here had the only one in the district, so I came up to grab it. I'm glad I saw you'.

'Why; do you want to sue me over your arm?'

'No, don't be silly, it's great. I wanted to talk to you about Ethel'.

'Well I'm on my way to the surgery now; would you like to come along?'

'If you're not too busy'.

Sandy surprised me, more than I could really appreciate. I could hardly believe what he told me. They had not consummated the marriage. I was stunned.

'How long have you been married now Sandy?'

'It's nearly eighteen months now'.

He had tears in his eyes. I was staggered. I had never been faced with this problem before. What should I do? How should I handle it? Two healthy young people, in love, what on earth could be the trouble?

He went on to tell me, in his own time, how he had approached Ethel. He tried nothing on the wedding night—they were both over-tired and he could understand her request. But the next afternoon, when he made approaches, she resisted. They were still in their Sydney hotel and were due to sail from Circular Quay at eight. Perhaps she was waiting for a special situation before she gave up her virginity. He thought he understood. Surely it would be all right on the ship, in the special deluxe cabin which would be theirs.

That first night on board was so exciting, meeting friends and having a few drinks and then the roughish Tasman Sea as they wobbled their way to the cabin, made Sandy unsure how to behave. Ethel said she felt queer, with the tossing and pitching of the ship, she just wanted to go to bed. They had single beds, of course, in the cabin, so he saw Ethel to bed and asked if she wanted anything for her queer feelings.

'No, I'll be OK. I just want to go to sleep. I hope it doesn't get too rough'.

The next day seemed steadier. The captain had his party to welcome all and afterwards they found they were seated at the captain's table. Those in the deluxe suite usually were.

Ethel seemed bright and happy; there were two other couples at the table. They all got on famously. One of the other couples were honeymooners also. The captain was going to enjoy this voyage. They were to go right across the Pacific, through the canal and disembark in Genoa.

Poor Sandy. He didn't know how to handle Ethel. Every day she had an excuse to protect her virginity. Did other chaps have this trouble? She became quite odd, almost hostile, when they were alone together, yet in company she was a different girl. What a happy couple they appeared. Poor Sandy—and poor Ethel really—they both had a problem.

Sandy went on to tell me so much about that honeymoon, of all his attempts with Ethel, all her excuses. She got to the stage when she would not even talk about it.

'But Sandy, surely you got into bed with her and fondled her, surely it must have led to something.'

'Yes, of course I did. She would let me get into bed and even get my arms around her and kiss her and all that, but when I got my hands down towards her she would stiffen up and pull away. She wouldn't let me touch even the hairs round her fanny. Then she would say she had a headache or some other excuse'.

'God, Sandy, this is dreadful. You have really shocked me'.

'Well I had to talk to someone Doc. I've worried and worried and tried and tried until I'm nearly mad. Having to keep it all to myself and keep up appearances has nearly driven me crazy. You're the only one I've spoken to about it. I don't know what you can do to help, but I'm glad I told you.

'Yes, I appreciate your faith. I shall not breathe a word of this to anyone, have no fear. I must think about it though, and I really must let you go now for I am late. Will you come and see me tomorrow night here, about 5.30 and we'll talk again?'

'Sure, I'll get here. I'm sorry I took up so much of your time, but I had to talk, Doc'.

'Of course you did, quite right, let me think about it, see you tomorrow'.

What a problem! What could I do now?

My first thought was back to what RM had said after the polo. She suspected something. Women are smart. Mine was anyway. I would have to talk to her. RM was privy to my innermost thoughts, even from our earliest days of marriage. She would never betray a trust—a perfect doctor's wife. She might even know the answer! I didn't.

We did discuss the problem that night in bed. I told her all Sandy had said. She listened quietly, saying very little, and shortly I heard the beginnings of those puffy little snores which indicated the end of that subject. What remarks she had made were not sympathetic to Ethel. RM had guessed something was the matter, women did have a sixth sense.

Sandy did get to the surgery a bit later than 5.30 the next afternoon. I had thought about his problem a lot during the day. I was really beginning to feel quite hostile towards Ethel, but before I allowed this feeling to take over I wanted to ask Sandy quite a bit more.

'Sorry I'm late Doc, things were hectic today. Have I kept you?'

'No, we can talk as long as you like now. I have finished'.

'I'm so relieved I met you yesterday morning and told you my troubles. I feel so much better; like having a friend on side with me now. I do hope you have some suggestions'.

'I don't know about any suggestions, but I have thought an awful lot about you today. Would you tell me a bit more so that perhaps some bright idea might come to me? Tell me exactly how you first made any deliberate attempt to deflower her'.

'Well, after about a week on the ship, we had left Auckland and were in that beautifully calm Pacific Ocean. We were enjoying our whole day, joining in all the excitements of shipboard life, except for our problem. I decided to bring the matter to a head. I felt I had to. It was no good letting it go for I felt the longer I did the worse it would get'.

'When we got to our cabin after watching a musical show and having a few drinks with friends afterwards, I told her, as we undressed, that she would just have to have intercourse with me. She began to cry saying she knew this time would come and she dreaded it. When I asked her why, she told me a long story, which she had never mentioned before, about an incident at boarding school, when she was about thirteen'.

'One of her teachers, who had always seemed so nice to her and always helped her with any of her problems, was the cause of it. The essence of the story was that on a long weekend, all the boarders had gone home except her, because her parents were overseas. This teacher behaved in a most unexpected and, what Ethel thought was, a most unusual way. She went to her room with her after playing draughts together for most of the evening and was watching her get undressed, when she began to fondle her. She was so persuasive that they lay down together and the teacher became very familiar and wanted Ethel to do the same. Ethel knew it was all wrong but didn't know how to handle the situation until she felt fingers being pushed into her vagina. She instinctively revolted, got up and locked herself in the bathroom. This episode has been on her mind ever since. She has bottled it up and never told anyone, not even her mother. Her relations with the teacher were very cool until she noticed her absence. They were all told she had left for another school'.

'She poured all this out, in between sobs, and said she just couldn't bear anyone to touch her there now'.

'So I went on to try and explain that this was long ago and she would have to forget it. She was married now and it would be quite different. I told her I could understand how she had been offended, but having a husband was quite a different matter from being fondled by a queer woman. We would have to learn about one another and begin to live a normal married life. She kept on sobbing as she nestled her head on my shoulder and eventually said she would try'.

He went on to explain that after they had had this talk he was sure things would be better and eventually all would be well. He did realise however that it could take time and be very tricky; he would have to be very gentle and caring.

She did permit some caressing, more than ever before. He was gentle. However when they rolled together and she felt how hard he was she stiffened up. Even though he tried to get her to handle him, she resisted.

And so his story went on—all over the Pacific. They talked and talked, but nothing was ever allowed to happen. He became angry, while she admitted she thought she never would be able to accept intercourse.

'God, Doc, imagine how I felt. Not only was I a failure, but I was in a disastrous situation. The marriage could never be a success. What was I to do? What would happen when we got home? Should I divorce her? How could we explain to our parents? I felt completely defeated'.

'Yes, of course. Do your parents know?'

'No. They only keep hoping to hear of a grandchild. This is what I want you to help me with. Should I tell them the truth now, or should we just go for a divorce, on the grounds of incompatibility?'

'Hold on; I'm not sure a divorce is the answer—yet. Surely there's something we can do before that. I hesitate to suggest it, and I would not look forward to it, but do you think Ethel would talk to me about her problem?'

'I'm not sure Doc. I suggested she should see someone, long ago, but she is difficult, and I'm sure she feels very ashamed of herself?'

Well, we could always shoot her off to a psychiatrist for hypnosis therapy if I cannot get through to her. Would she agree, do you think?'

'You'd have to ask her. I have, but never really got any proper answer'.

'Sandy have you tried any really strong man stuff?'

'What do you mean Doc?'

'What about gin? How would it be if you got her ''tipsy'' and even a bit more, then put her down and then forced your way in? After all, this must have happened before and if she is almost unconscious and you are strong and firm, it may be quite a show, but it may work. If you forcefully raped her, she would surely know it. She may even welcome this strong man approach to solve her problem. What do you think?'

'I don't know. I suppose I could organise it, but afterwards, do you

70

think she would be worse or better? I suppose there is a risk here'.

'Yes. I'm not sure Sandy. The female mind is such an enigma that I wouldn't like to guess which way the cat would jump. I'm not convinced that any psychiatrist could predict this with certainty, either'.

'I'll think about it Doc. Ethel doesn't drink much so I'll have to plan something. I'll let you know. Also I ought to let you get home to dinner'.

'Why not come around and have dinner with us? I'm sure Rosemarie would be pleased to see you, and Elsie always has a nice dinner'. 'No thank you, I told Ethel I would be home for dinner!' 'I'd better get back. I'll keep in touch. Thanks so much for all your time'.

Sandy did consider what I suggested and he did plan it. The whole affair was a disaster, not only because Ethel was resistant to drinking much alcohol, but also she considered it an attack, which she resisted with force. She had not spent years handling difficult horses for nothing.

Ethel, who really wanted to overcome her problem, did agree to visit a psychiatrist, after two long conversations with me. I had spent the best part of two hours listening to her story, most of which I knew by now, before I was able to get my views over to her. I pointed out, with some firmness, that marriage and intercourse were integral. There could be no separating the two. She had been unwise and even deceitful to get married, knowing what she knew about herself. I avoided creating tears, but not by much. She asked about the hypnosis therapy which would be offered to her. I strongly recommended she undergo whatever her psychiatrist suggested.

They both went off to Sydney with a long referral letter from me to Dr Sinclair-Burke, whom I found out had some success with this sort of problem. She had a long course of hypnotic suggestion until Dr S-B declared that they should now go home and try to live a natural married life. He had advised against any attempts at intercourse while undergoing treatment, which advice they took.

I received a long case report from Dr Sinclair-Burke telling me all that he had discovered about Ethel's past and how he had tried to 'exorcise the devil' with a course of hypnosis. He did agree that her trouble seemed to be very deep rooted (literally)! which made the prognosis unfavourable. However, he had done all that was possible.

When Sandy came to see me shortly after they arrived home he told me there was no sign of any improvement. He and Ethel had finally agreed to a divorce and they would now tell the parents the whole story.

Both families were shattered. They had no idea of the situation but accepted the mutual decison for the divorce. They all agreed that the true facts should not be allowed to escape, while they felt so sorry for both Ethel and Sandy and the whole saga.

Ethel eventually moved to another district in Southern NSW, where she developed a horse stud with much success.

She became a recluse. Progeria was evident and one can only imagine how her neurosis affected her mind. In spite of her physical decline she managed a horse breeding programme which produced many winners in metropolitan races. It would be only speculation to suggest that the servicing of her mares by selected stallions gave her some type of inverted satisfaction for her own failing.

She must have suffered so much. Perhaps when her premature ageing led to her death in the 1960s, she at last experienced peace, the first since that long weekend at boarding school.

Sandy remarried two years after the divorce, had a happy life and four children.

Ethel's life was a tragedy, far more than just one of infertility. With this tragedy in mind it seems not inappropriate to end this true story with another . . . in a lighter vein.

This story concerns a Belgian diplomat, whose English was very poor. At an international meeting he encountered one of his English friends who enquired about the Belgian's wife, who incidentally, had no children after some years of marriage.

'Oh, thank you she is well, but . . . you know . . . how you say it . . . she is unbearable.'

Seeing the look of surprise on his friend's face the Belgian went on . . . 'Oh pardon me . . . my English, she is no good . . . I mean . . . my wife . . . she is inconceivable'.

The friend still looking shattered, the Belgian again apologised . . . 'Oh, I am sorry . . . what I really mean is . . . she is insurmountable.'

Just like Ethel? . . . No!!

CHAPTER TWELVE

Mistaken Gender

I had called in to the surgery, after hospital rounds, about eleven in the morning. This happened most mornings. By then the mail would have been brought in by someone and it was about time for a cup of tea.

Out in the workroom Mabs could always be found moving about her duties; perhaps a dressing or removing some sutures, watching those having shortwave diathermy, whatever it was, there was always the happy greeting—'Good morning, and how are you this morning.' I heard this so often, forty years ago, that it can still be recalled most crisply.

We would usually fit in a cup and often Walter would arrive about now with his greeting—'Now doctor, what are you up to.' His habit was always to call me ''doctor'' in a sort of ''official'' way and this is still so even today, except when we are alone.

Our receptionist, Molly, would often come out when we were all together and tell us of some house calls that had been requested and we would discuss these, often exchanging a bit of gossip or advice such as, 'Now Doctor, when you open the gate remember it usually falls off' or 'Don't stay longer than you have to, remember the neighbours watch' or 'If those cats are in the way, kick them in the teeth'' as Walter would imitate his 'kicking cats' routine. We did enjoy Walt's humour.

Molly came back to say there was a call for me. It was Sergeant Bedingfield to tell me that old Jim McClew had come into the station this morning to tell him his pal, Paddy Sploggs, 'didn't seem too good.' In fact he couldn't get him to move and thought he might be dead. Would I go out to their camp and investigate?

Jim and Paddy were known as a couple who had lived together out in a hut along the Bunnan Road, about eight miles from town. They would sometimes get a job helping out on nearby farms, but with no ability except of manual labour, and just as little enthusiasm, they would not be sought except in extraordinary circumstances. Jim looked about sixty, but I was told it was hard to know Paddy's age. They were always dressed in old creaseless baggy trousers, grey flannel shirts and ill-fitting coats. Even on summer days the coats would be worn, if they were in town.

Their visits to town were usually only on every second Friday when they called at the post office to collect the welfare cheques. So they were not really well known. They did not visit any of the five hotels except to collect their flagons of port and sweet sherry from the bottle departments.

This was all told to me by Sergeant Bedingfield to whom I had to admit I could not recall ever seeing either of them. He told me he considered them as 'no-hopers', certainly 'non payers', so would I mind going out to see what had happened?

There was a broken down gate in a fence just about opposite the 'Yarrandi' homestead on the Bunnan Road. Although I had passed there many times I did not remember ever having seen it. However, I found it which then led me into a treed paddock, with a track leading up a moderate grade, to the foothills. The track was not well worn but was sufficient to follow as I wondered where it would lead.

Within about four hundred yards I suddenly came upon a dilapidated small iron shed and as I approached, several barking dogs came rushing up to my car. There was no other sign of life.

I got out of my car, was brave enough to pat a couple of the dogs and walked slowly towards the hut which was only a one-roomed affair about twenty by twelve feet, with a rusty water tank alongside it. It was heavily surrounded by small miserable looking gum trees so that it could certainly never be seen from the main road.

I looked around, expecting to see or hear someone, but instead I got the impression of an odd eeriness. I slowly walked to the one entrance on the upside of the hut and looked in.

There was no order apparent, the floor was dirt, a few empty tins and other rubbish led my eyes to an improvised couch of hessian on boxes. On this was a body lying supine. It was clothed in baggy trousers, boots and an ill-fitting coat. The head would have been bald if many long strands of temporal hair had not been trained up and over the crown.

My 'Good-day' fell on deaf ears, or as I expected, on dead ears.

That cold blueness of a dead face had already set in. I lifted the left arm, the nearest one, and found it stiff and cold and very dead. I lifted up an eyelid which showed a glassy lustreless eye before it very slowly closed again. There was no breathing and no radial pulse. He was dead. He had probably been so for some hours. The local flies had already agreed and were moving in as they usually do on dead bodies.

For protocol's sake I put my stethoscope down over the base of the neck and of course there was silence.

I could do nothing. I walked outside and called loudly 'Hullo' not knowing whether to expect an answer or a bullet. The whole scene was eerie. I thought it best to get out and back to town. I got into my car and started up and was about to leave when something told me to go back and have a further look. After all there may have been some evidence of

Paddy Sploggs didn't seem too good...

a bullet wound or other injuries. So I would go back and look more thoroughly.

I opened the coat buttons and pulled up the grey flannel shirt to find a very thin body with a scaphoid abdomen and the chest showed poorly covered ribs. I listened again to the heart. All was silent. But I did notice what I thought was an excessive skin fold over the heart. I looked again, there was certainly excess skin there. I looked over the right side, the same excessive loose skin was there.

This seemed odd in an emaciated man. So I opened up the buttons of the fly and there I found a female distribution of pubic hair over female genitalia.

I covered up the area again, pulled down the shirt, and this time decided to get back and tell Sergeant Bedingfield all I had learnt.

That night the Sydney evening papers had this headline

YOUNG DOCTOR SAYS * 'THIS MAN IS A WOMAN'

It was, of course, what I had told the sergeant and because the press was short of news they took up this story. Scone was on the map!

The sergeant had known these two for some time and was shocked to learn that Paddy was a woman.

The body was brought in by ambulance. Toby Barton was asked to do the autopsy by the Coroner (Mr Seaward) and an inquest was held. The internal organs were sent to Sydney for examination but revealed no unusual findings. The Coroner found no apparent cause of death so an open finding was returned. Jim was distraught and could add little to the enquiry. He was illiterate, mentally weak and was judged to be innocent by the Coroner. No charge would be laid. Death was due to 'causes unknown'.

The district was interested and intrigued by the story and the disclosure but was otherwise not disturbed.

An odd, and apparently harmless but loving relationship was revealed with no one being greatly moved by the whole affair, except Jim.

What happened to him we do not know. He moved from the district and could not be traced.

Today in any large city the clothing rarely helps to indicate the wearer's sex. In 1947, trousers meant a man!

CHAPTER THIRTEEN

A Lesson in Contraception

General practice throughout Australia in the forties included what were called 'lodge' patients. The lodges or Friendly Societies, of which there were several, made contractural arrangements (CFA or Common Form of Agreement) with practitioners to treat their members for a fee structure which was less than the consultation and other service fees usually charged to non 'lodge' patients. Lodge members were able to approach their secretary and request to be put on the medical scheme. They would pay a quarterly fee to the secretary which would entitle the member and his wife, and children under the age of 14 years, to free medical treatment excluding confinements and surgical operations. Hospital treatment for medical rather than surgical conditions was covered by the contract. The lodges had a similar arrangement with chemists, who would supply goods at greatly reduced rates to members and their families.

The fees paid by members of these Friendly Societies or 'lodges' for medical coverage were 26 shillings per annum in the cities, and 32 shillings in the country. The secretary would provide the doctor with a list of members every three months, with a cheque to cover those on the list for the previous three months.

Some practices, in those years, consisted mainly of lodge patients, while others had smaller lists depending on the suburb or district, and also on whether the doctor wished to have lodge patients.

A lodge member, whose income exceeded £260 pa at the time of his initiation to the lodge, was not entitled to medical benefits, however after joining, his income could rise to £364 pa before he would be excluded from the medical benefits list.

As the youngest doctor in Scone in 1940 I welcomed lodge patients while Walter was equally happy to hand over his lodge lists to me. The secretary of each of the three lodges in Scone were notified of this and after they approved of my appointment as their lodge doctor, I had a sizable nucleus for my practice. My surgery door was always open to these lodge patients and visits to their homes were made free of charge. As a general rule these arrangements were satisfactory and honestly conducted. Unnecessary calls were rare.

The fees for a confinement, including all ante-and post-natal care was four guineas for lodge patients and six guineas for private patients. Minor operations ranged from one to three guineas, while majors ranged from twelve to eighteen for lodge patients and fifteen to twenty-five for private patients. Anaesthetic fees were one guinea for minor operations and three guineas for major operations.

These lodge arrangements were unaltered when I returned from the war in 1946.

Mrs Buckingham was a lodge patient. She lived with her husband and seven children in the gatekeeper's house just out of town on one of the railway crossings. Mr Buckingham worked as a fettler on the railways which meant that his wife was responsible for 'keeping the gates'. Whenever a train was approaching this railway crossing, she had to go out from the little house and close off the two gates to the road. There were, in 1946, on average, about fifty-five trains passing through Scone each day which meant Mrs Buckingham spent a large portion of her day opening and closing two heavy gates.

The seventh child of this union had been born in 'Brancaster' about three weeks before I was brought a message that Mrs Buckingham wanted me to make a call out to the gates. A police constable brought me this message.

'Is it urgent?' He wasn't sure, but got the impression that the call concerned the baby.

'OK, I'll get out there as soon as I can. There are three patients left in the waiting room so I should be there within an hour'.

'Thank you doctor, I'll let my sergeant know', as he left.

The gates were a few miles out of Scone at the turn-off to the homestead. I pulled off the main road and left my car on the dirt road just alongside the gatekeeper's cottage. It was the usual small dwelling provided for gatekeepers by the NSW Government Railways, always built at these road crossings and within a few feet of the railway track. A more unsuitable situation in which to house and bring up seven children would be hard to imagine, especially as the husband was away working for five days a week.

I entered through a small broken hinged gate in a wire fence and immediately almost fell over a tricycle at the entrance to the house. It was not my first visit so I was well prepared for the shambles I knew I would meet. The baby was crying, the three pre-school children with two ill-fed dogs were clustered around Mrs Buckingham, sitting on a rickety kitchen chair trying its best not to collapse under her weight. She was trying to get the new baby, which I had delivered, or should I say, which delivered itself, three weeks earlier, to take to her large exposed left breast. Walter had told me that after her first confinement, several years earlier, he had never got to be present at the others. She always had them so quickly—a doctor's delight.

'What's the matter Mrs Buckingham. Can't you get it to feed?'

'Oh, it seems to take it all right doctor, but it won't keep it down. Soon after I came home from hospital it started vomiting after every feed. It's hardly dirtying its nappy and I'm sure it's losing weight.'

Just then we heard a distant train whistle.

'Oh, my God, it's the three-forty; the gates'.

I told her to stay where she was. I rushed out, with the small kids and the dogs after me, and managed to get the gates open for the train. They should have been closing off the road but earlier she had rushed into her baby, after opening them, and forgotten to close them.

As I stood there the steam engine rushed past making lots of important noises, blowing steam from its piston and filthy soot from its funnel. Miraculously, the children and the dogs knew the drill for survival, and kept back from certain death.

I got back into the house after the long goods train had passed and the gate situation was restored. After all that noise I wondered why any of the Buckingham family kept their food down, when this happened fifty-five times a day. On reflection, I expect it was because there was not much food available. The husband's wages were £4-2-6 per week, the then basic wage paid to the fettlers. Perhaps there was a little more for the gatekeeping, but I think the rent free house was supposed to compensate for that.

How these women managed always amazed me. The house furniture was basic, brown linoleum on the floor, dusty muslin curtains at the windows on the trainline side of the house, rickety old iron bedsteads with unmade bedclothes, kerosene hurricane lamps for night light, all housed in this small iron roofed fibrous walled house, with the usual outside lavatory.

Her husband would bring most of their supplies home on his fettlers hand trolley at night after work. They obviously just managed on his wage, no doubt using mainly basic foods. Bread was then 2½d a loaf and milk 1½d a pint.

However, my problem was the new baby. I realised it was sick and I could do nothing for it here. I told Mrs Buckingham she would have to let me take it back to the hospital and examine it properly. I would send out the town ambulance with a nurse as soon as I got back to Scone.

'What about your breast milk?' I enquired.

'Oh, don't worry about that doctor. That won't cause me any trouble. Young Billy is still using it'.

I looked at young Billy, with his six teeth and a large smile on his dirty face, no doubt due to his anticipated sole ownership of all that milk.

'How often does Billy get a drink?'

'Quite often, whenever I have time to sit down'.

'Do his teeth hurt you?'

'Lord no doctor, even young Tim, the next one, sometimes has a drink. You know I have never dried up since my first, and he's now twelve. I'll have the baby ready for the ambulance. You're sure you'll be able to fix it doctor. She's the only girl I've got'.

'I'll certainly do my best to find out what's wrong, and I'll call out sometime tomorrow and let you know'.

As I drove back the few miles I felt sorry that people had to live like that. I realised I would not get paid for my attention and would go back and cancel the four guineas on her account card for the recent confinement. Perhaps 'Brancaster' would get a few shillings in due course but I doubted that too.

We found Mrs Buckingham's story of the constant vomiting after meals quite accurate. At the time, I was convinced that the baby had a pyloric stenosis. The story seemed to fit the diagnosis, except for one thing. The vomiting was not always projectile. My limited experience, firstly as a medical student and secondly with a recent case which I had to deal with, seemed to require a definite projectile component to the vomiting before a sure diagnosis of pyloric stenosis could be made. I don't know why this is so, but it suggests the muscular action around the pyloric part of the duodenum is unbalanced. This suggestion can be supported by the fact that a simple operation which partly cuts through most of the circular muscle fibres, cures the problem. I had done one, only a few weeks before, with a successful outcome, more to my surprise than the parents'. This was the first and only Ramsteadt's operation that I ever did.

Perhaps this success went to my head. Perhaps I was hoping for another opportunity to do a second. However as we observed Baby Buckingham I could not be convinced that a pyloric stenosis was the correct diagnosis. Sister Batterham suggested a weaker milk mixture, and her clever manipulations over the next three weeks saw the baby start to gain weight and stop all vomiting.

Why Mrs Buckingham's breast milk was unacceptable to this baby and not to the others, was a mystery to me. This was her only girl. Was this the reason?!!!

Mrs Buckingham was so grateful to have her baby girl back and a week later her husband came up to my surgery one evening with a large chocolate sponge cake.

We discussed his future prospects with the NSW Government Railways in which he hoped to progress to become a guard, and later, even a signalman. He obviously was a trier. I think he was glad I showed interest in his prospects for he went on to say he would like to ask me something personal. He plucked up courage to tell me that he didn't want any more children but that he found he could not lie with his wife and not desire sexual intercourse. 'How can we prevent more children?' was his question.

As medical students we were given one lecture on the question of contraception in our fifth year. Our lecturer had talked of the early attempts at contraception from the days of Cleopatra onwards. We were told how camel owners put marbles into the wombs of their camels to prevent them becoming pregnant—a happening which no doubt would be a disaster to the Sahara transport services and a useless, but well remembered, piece of information for a medical student. We were told of old fashioned attempts at douching immediately after intercourse, at having intercourse with a pepper shaker alongside the orgasmal couch so that the woman could be made to sneeze violently after the event, in the hope that the sperms would be discouraged from entering the womb.

A popular more 'recent' method was the use of a sponge, such as we used to clean our slates at school. This should have a string attached and the sponge should be soaked in vinegar for twelve hours before intercourse. It should then be placed in the depths of the vagina just before the event. One should make sure that the string was left hanging out so that the vinegar soaked sponge could easily be removed and tidied up for the next time. We were not informed of the effect of vinegar on the male organ!

We were told of another method of doubtful use namely of having the woman, immediately after intercourse, get up on a chair and jump to the ground at least twelve times.

The woman was undoubtedly the disadvantaged in all these methods. What about the male, could he be asked to help?

There were, in my learning days at the university, three avenues open to the male.

Firstly: no intercourse at all was the safest, the accepted norm in our society!

Secondly: he could withdraw his penis before ejaculation. This was obviously unreliable.

Thirdly: he could wear a sheath or condom.

If the man could be relied on to wear a condom and if the condom was not faulty and only one intercourse were to occur then this method was the safest known and could be recommended. There was a widely accepted rumour that legislation was in place for condom manufacturers to ensure that one in ten was faulty, which made them acceptable to those who enjoyed Russian roulette!!

Now, having ruminated over all these thoughts, I decided that the sheath would be what I should recommend to Ted Buckingham. All the other methods required much organisation and co-operation between the partners, and knowing the intellectual level of both Mr and Mrs Buckingham and their situation in the little cottage, with trains rushing by so close to their double bed, I had no doubt that the condom was for them. There would now be no more children. I was sure he would get a considerable discount from the chemist, as he was on lodge benefits.

So, in answer to his question as to how to stop children, I told him about condoms.

'What are they, Doc?'

'They're a sort of cover you put over yourself before you get into bed with your wife'.

'But we got covers Doc'.

'Not that sort Ted, what I mean is a cover for your "old man". You may have heard of them as "French letters".'

'Augh them, yeah, I've never seen one but I've heard me mates talk about them'.

'Well, they're pretty safe and should do the trick for you'.

So I sent him off to Mr Barnett to get a supply of condoms.

Next day he was back; he wanted to see me to make sure he knew how to use them properly.

'The chemist just gave me these three packets and I don't see any instructions on them'.

'Oh you should know how to use them Ted. You just roll them on beforehand'.

He opened up one packet and I could see he had been looking at them because they were all loose. I picked one up and rolled it back to its original state, with the little ballooned tip in the centre.

'Now', I said 'you just roll it back down over yourself until it's out to its full length'.

'Oh I tried, but I couldn't get it straight. I tell you what Doc, while you've been telling me this and I've been watching you handle it, I've suddenly got a "hard". Would you mind putting it on for me so's I'll know properly how to do it?'

Well now, this was a situation I had not expected and had never faced before. In my surprised state the next thing I witnessed was Ted undoing his fly buttons and out came his large erect penis. Large would not do it justice. Huge or even enormous, would be more appropriate. I had never seen such a 'whopper'. I imagined the amount of blood it must have taken from his general circulation to fill it and to create such a tumesence. It amazed me that such an amount of blood being diverted from his other bodily requirements, especially blood flow to his brain, had not caused him to faint, due to its lack of oxygen. My thoughts even went further as I wondered if there were not research possibilities here concerning the relationship between the size of the male penis and the intellect!!! Did men with enormous organs, often in use, deprive their brains of oxygen and so have lower IQs? Maybe this could be a future thesis for a Doctorate of Medicine.

Anyway, back to my situation. There I was, with a condom in my hand, staring at Ted's enormous erect organ.

'Go on Doc, show me how to put it on'.

So, as the door of the surgery was firmly closed and I knew no one could see what I was about to do, I put the condom over the head of his penis and attempted to roll it down. From the start I was aware that it would take some doing. I doubted I could do it. I had found out during my early training days in the army, when given the job of testing condoms, that they had great expansile qualities. But that was when they were filled with water. Could I now stretch this one over Ted's penis? It reminded me of the days when I used to mend punctures in the tubes of my 'baby Austin' wheels; tyre levers were necessary to urge the tyre back on to the wheel. Would I need some sort of lever here to get the wretched thing over his penis?

I asked him to hold one side down while I stretched the opposite side to try and get it started. It flipped out of our fingers, as we lost control when it was under tension. It flew off on to the floor under my desk.

What on earth was I doing in this situation?!!! Was this what a country general practitioner was supposed to do? I had to do something. Ted had asked for help and furthermore I had advised this method. I couldn't abandon my suggestion now.

I wondered if there were various sizes of condoms. I phoned Mr Barnett the chemist for advice on this matter. As far as he knew they were all the same size but he admitted he was not really sure; he had never had occasion to study this question. He had never been asked before. We went on to discuss the problem I was dealing with in my surgery which seemed to have a disturbing effect on him. After a long pause he regained his composure and asked if I had tried any form of lubricant.

'What would you suggest I try?'

'Have you got any Vaseline or zinc cream in your room? Why not try something like that?'

So we started again. Ted remained at 'attention' all the while I was speaking with the chemist.

I got the Vaseline jar and smeared some all over the head of his organ. The whole procedure disgusted me; so out of context in my life as a GP. Anyway I felt I had to continue towards some solution.

As we started again, Ted, holding one rim of the condom and I on the opposite side of the rim, told him to pull down with me and at the same time to give a push.

Hooray, hooray, it stretched over and I quickly rolled it down to its full extent. It covered only half the length of his penis when Ted got a fixed stare on his face and made a couple of grunting noises. The inevitable had happened. Thank goodness the sheath was there to protect me and my surgery furniture. Soon the subsidence began. I quickly told him to leave the condom on and dress himself and leave me to my next patient.

With pride I made my parting remark—'Now you know how to get it on; don't forget to use one every time'.

I needed some time to recover my senses. What an experience! I had to go along and tell Walter what I had been doing. His sense of humour took up the cue. The end result of his flights of amused imaginings with their endless possibilities, particularly if it were known what I had done and what we had discussed was a decision to have a model made. We would keep such a phallic artwork far back in our lower drawer, away from Sister's eyes. The need for different sizes could be overcome by having our carpenter make an expanding type with a thumbscrew up the middle, somewhat like mother's old fashioned shoe stretchers.

After two cups of tea and much mirth, the cause intrigued Sister because we could not tell her all, not yet anyway, later perhaps because she was sure to find our model!

That night as I reflected on the day's performance, I was surprised at myself. I really didn't expect events (or the condom) to unfold as they did. I almost despised myself for becoming so involved in a way which I found disgusting. My only solace was that I had been led into it (by the hand) because of my offer to help when asked. To me it was reminiscent of those other ridiculous occasions in my early days in the army when as the MO, I was obliged to conduct 'short arm parades'. Whether this illogical and disgusting relic of British military discipline still exists in today's army, I have no idea. For those in doubt, a 'short arm parade' was one in which all members of the unit were required to parade, standing 'at ease', with flies undone and penises held exposed, on which the medical officer was expected to pass judgment on the presence or otherwise of gonorrhoea.

This practice was not only quite unscientific as a means of making such a diagnosis, but to me was abhorrent. In the many camps in which I was obliged to conduct such parades I deliberately walked along the lines with my eyes closed, often finding I had wandered off course by rubbing against the objects for inspection, some soft and some hard! I can only hope the Australian Army has abandoned such a ludicrous practice. The Japanese, whose guest I became for four years were not so highly civilised, so they missed out on this indignity—about the only one.

I satisfied my discomforting thoughts with the hope that my efforts would prevent any further babies for the gatekeeper.

Six months went by when one Saturday morning Ted Buckingham came to see me just before my surgery closed. He looked frightfully upset, so I made him sit down.

'Goodness, what's the matter with you?'

He hung his head and began to cry. It was obviously very difficult for him to speak. Eventually he burst out,

'She's gone again.'

'What do you mean? Who's gone again?'

'My wife, she's in the family way again?'

'Now, how could that happen? Haven't you been using the sheath?'

'Yes doctor, I promise, every time'.

So I asked him further about it. The only relevant fact I was able to get was that the children had found a packet some months back and when he came home from work one day he found them out in the backyard trying to blow them up, while the cat watched this new game with interest and an occasional pat with its paw. He hurriedly took the three condoms, rolled them up and put them back in the packet and hid them. This evidence led me to suspect that one must have suffered and was therefore the culprit in this condom drama.

CHAPTER FOURTEEN

The Lows and Highs of General Practice

Social life was as enjoyable as that of medical practice. As a doctor one not only entered most of the surrounding homesteads when illness struck but dinner invitations came in happier times.

Most families preferred their doctor to call personally when one of them was sick rather than make the trip to town. For the doctor these visits were mostly pleasant affairs for it meant a drive out of town, a pleasant reception at the homestead and into the sick room, usually tidied and dressed for the occasion, a chair by the bedside while the history was taken and a hovering relative to answer any of the doctor's needs. A good history would usually point fairly directly to the diagnosis; in the winter time, chest ailments prevailed while abdominal pains were perennial. Whatever the story and the examination revealed, the withdrawal to the sitting room for tea, sandwiches and cakes was the ritual setting for discussion. After explanation of the trouble the treatment would be discussed. It may be that medicines would be dispensed and dispatched from town with instructions and advice about nursing details and further visits, or it may be necessary to break the news gently that more serious procedures were indicated, a visit to the hospital for an operation or even in rare cases the request for a visit by a Sydney specialist. We had many close colleagues, in most specialties, who would be able to arrange these country visits. Sometimes they would drive the 200 miles, sometimes they would brave a charter flight in a small aeroplane.

There were occasions when a leading neurosurgeon would come for head injuries and operate in our local Scott Memorial Hospital. Such visits were red carpet affairs by all involved at the hospital. One of us would assist at the operation, the other would administer the anaesthesia. Head and spine injuries were not uncommon in this horse and grazing district.

There was one visit by a Macquarie Street physician to the wife of the owner of one of the largest and oldest properties in the district. Walter

86

was away which was not to my advantage as he had been their own beloved doctor for many years. The wife had a pneumonia which my ministrations of oxygen and penicillin were not controlling. She was very sick and I got that 'gut' feeling, which only doctors get, of an impending disaster. I quickly advised the relatives that I wanted a specialist's opinion. The weather for light aircraft flying over the ranges to Scone meant he would drive.

The protocol of such visits was always observed. I would meet the visiting specialist, outline the story and the treatment given so far and of course a bit about the family. The visitor would be introduced to the relatives, usually in Matron's office, where a short conversation would precede my leading him to the bedside where an appropriate introduction would be made. A few remarks, then a look at the chart and medical notes, interspersed with a few words with the sister standing by, then the examination followed by a few words with the patient would all be conducted with decorum and in no haste.

Next, the specialist would precede me out of the room when the two of us would have a private discussion of the case and what should be done. This could take some time after which the relatives would again be met when the specialist would explain in detail the diagnosis, the treatment to date, any tests required, the future treatment and the prognosis. He would answer all their questions. The whole procedure was time consuming but of great comfort to the relatives to know that all possible was being done and in the most civilised way, whatever the predicted outcome. It was a comfort to me to know that a higher authority had been introduced to this worrying situation. This personal visit by the specialist would always be followed up with daily phone calls for progress reports and for adjusting therapies.

This method of consultation, operating in the pre-war years and early post-war years was satisfactory to all and compassionate for the relatives. Such a visit to Scone would cost between £200 and £250. This was expensive and obviously reserved for those who could afford it. However, for those in trouble who could not afford it, we would always ring our appropriate colleague in Sydney for advice which offered considerable comfort to the relatives. This advice was willingly given— without charge.

This particular case of pneumonia proved to be a new variant of an old disease, caused by a virus, not a bacillus. Penicillin was of no value in its treatment. Although new antibiotics were being brought on to the market in rapid succession in the late 1940s, there seemed to be none effective for this viral type of pneumonia. This woman, aged forty-six, died in spite of all our efforts. My premonition had come true—again.

Apart from this 'gut' feeling I had learnt to recognise, which was so often right, I wondered if there were a psychic element in it. I first became aware of this 'horror' feeling during the war years. Suddenly the fear would come into my thoughts—'this chap is going to die'. The thought would come so suddenly. I dreaded it. Sometimes it was wrong, thankfully, but often it was right.

I suppose in this present case another factor was operating which may have helped produce this premonition. This woman, who came from interstate, had married into this old established grazing family of the Upper Hunter.

If ever a family suffered unfairly, this one did. One misfortune followed another. No family does, or should, pass through generations unscathed, yet some families seem to suffer more than the average. The misfortunes of this family seemed never ending. For the sake of anonymity all names have been changed and the timing of some events altered. The reasons for this are obvious, while the intent is to show how the life of the country doctor can enter so completely and emotionally into the family.

This family of Talbots was prolific but in no way ostentatious. The property was about 25 miles out of town, known as 'Silverton Hills' since its first settlement. There were five boys and three girls; a not unusual number of children for parents of the Victorian era. Only two of these children, on their way through life, could have been considered to have had average problems. This is their story.

In the first instance the mother was not only the child bearer but was the lynch pin. Her husband, endowed with much wealth, could unfortunately afford to be an alcoholic.

Whatever the cause, which remained unknown, 'Silverton Hills' was the scene of a fire when most of the homestead was destroyed and with it the first boy, James. He was burnt to death at the age of eight. The second boy, Simon, was burnt but saved from death by a neighbour. His permanent tattoo marks were those of his elastic garters, burnt into the skin of his calves. This was recorded on his army records. Also recorded was the note that following enemy action he was reported as 'missing' and never found.

The third boy grew to early adulthood. A healthy well built fair haired chap consulted Walter just prior to the war, with joint pains. In spite of all efforts to treat these he became crippled with rheumatoid arthritis until he became completely immobilised and died at the age of 39.

Harry, the fourth in line, was an active worker on the large property and was regarded as the one healthy and experienced son to manage the estate. He came in one evening after a not unusual day out mustering, said to his wife he felt tired, and died aged 40. The death certificate recorded the cause of death as 'coronary occlusion'.

His wife was my patient, whose death from an unsual type of viral pneumonia, occurred a year later.

The second of the girls, Millie, was an attractive girl who had schooled as a boarder in Sydney for five years, passed her leaving examination and had returned home for Christmas 1938. She had learnt to ride as a young girl and naturally spent hours in the saddle when home, helping the men on the property and was even useful at breaking in horses and selecting polo ponies for her remaining brother. On New Year's Eve she had been visiting neighbours for lunch and failed to return by 6 pm. A search found her unconscious alongside a large fallen tree which she always jumped when on that track.

She suffered a severe depressed skull fracture. Walter called his Sydney neurosurgeon colleague who, on New Year's Day 1939, operated upon her, doing all that was possible, short of replacing the large area of damaged brain.

Millie, for the rest of her life remained physically disabled'. Her speech was indecipherable, except by those closest to her, and her mobility was such that a permanent nurse was required until her death not so many years ago.

The fifth boy, Tony, tall, quiet and good looking, escaped the tragic events of his sibs and alone survived to manage the estate.

The first of the girls, the second oldest of the family, had a relatively uneventful upbringing and schooling. Her marriage seemed normal enough until the first confinement when she delivered twins. One grew up normally and developed into a brilliant student and an outstanding personality, the other was subnormal from birth and at fifteen years of age disappeared, never to be found.

This same mother, when she was forty-six years old consulted me for amenorrhoea, thought to be an early menopause, but which ended in the birth of a female. This child, when eighteen months old was brought into my surgery, walked up to me, put out her hand and said 'How do you do'. Used as I was to the extremes of this family, a feather would have knocked me down on the spot.

The eighth child of this unfortunate family of Talbots was a girl. She progressed fairly normally through childhood and teenage when at twenty she began having 'nervous breakdowns', one following the other at about year intervals. So she too joined the list of disasters.

Few families, in my experience, have suffered such a succession of tragedies. However, in general practice, especially in the country, the doctor became involved in most families and was introduced to their problems, not only the medical ones, which meant that compassion was as important, or more so, than expert medical knowledge. Without compassion one may have survived as a general practitioner in a country district but not with the fulfilment that was offered. The city practitioner could never quite experience the same fulfilment because he was not operating in such a closed community.

Not all visits to country homesteads were Aesculapian. The young doctor, back from the war, with a new and attractive wife, received many invitations. The doctor's day was full with many unexpected events to interrupt the planned program. Confinements, with their associated problems, always had priority. Farm accidents were frequent, while other urgent calls all added up to much frustration in the social scene. So many times Rosemarie would be ready, waiting to leave for a dinner party, when the phone would ring. Walter and I tried our best to prevent upsets to our plans and were mostly successful but even the best of plans in a busy practice would go wrong. Confinements were very personal affairs, and I was responsible for about 150 a year. There were many occasions when I would have to leave RM out in a country home at dinner while I had to go back to town, hoping that my return would not be too delayed.

We were invited to a large ball at 'Belltrees' to see in the New Year of 1948. RM, still in her early twenties, and one of the youngest wives, by now had got to know many of the district's personalities. As I parked my Vauxhall coupe in the large paddock, set aside for the purpose, RM commented on the huge number of guests. She was wearing a very pretty organdie dress printed in pink, blue, green and coral flowers with a frill around the bottom and the top. Fine pink velvet shoulder straps set off the flight of small pink bows down the front of the dress.

'Do stick by me. I always feel nervous in these big crowds, and I don't remember who everyone is'.

Just as I replied, 'Sure, don't worry, I'll be there', a short fattish woman and her husband caught up with us on the long coir matting which was leading us to the house when I heard, 'Here's the doctor and his pretty wife' at the same time as I heard RM's whisper, 'Who?', which I had no chance of answering as they were up with us.

'How are you dear? I haven't seen you since we met at Betty Halliday's some months ago. I don't suppose you remember me?'

RM surprised me, but not as much as she surprised her questioner, or, more so, herself.

'I'm very well Mrs Riddle, how are you?'

Mrs Riddle was so impressed that she spent most of that New Year's eve telling the other women of the district how clever she thought Rosemarie was to remember her, after only one meeting.

The old homestead at Belltrees had been the setting for many a magnificent occasion. Jim and Judy White received us as we moved into the gracious rooms which were already crowded with guests from near and far. RM and I stuck together for a while until the champagne took over and her confidence rose. She was learning about herself. The war years in Adelaide, as she approached adult life, were socially restrictive. Large parties such as the Belltrees New Year's eve ball were now re-emerging

We dined in the main rooms and after coffee moved to the woolshed where the band, warming up towards midnight, hotted up towards daylight. The woolshed floor and the rhythm of the orchestra turned night into day. What a marvellous party.

We made our farewells with the dawn appearing over the eastern ranges. As we started off on our drive back to Scone, with RM relaxed alongside me, making contented sighing noises, I said to her, 'Well you're a smarty pants. How the hell did you remember her name?'

'A flash of magic. When she spoke to me I had no idea what her name was although I could remember her face. I just opened my mouth and out came "Mrs Riddle".'

This was not the first time RM had made a mark. She was an intelligent girl whose mother had tried to teach her the social graces.

Rosemarie's mother had also attempted to teach her bridge, forecasting that it would be a social necessity of the future. She was quite right in her forecast although she often expressed her exasperation.

'Why was I given such a fool for a daughter?' when RM failed in some way to measure up to her mother's standard. My mother-in-law was a very dramatic person, and I loved her.

This parental attitude was probably the reason why my attempts to encourage RM to take to the bridge table met an icy reception.

In my POW days Jack Rymill and Geoff Gregory were responsible for teaching me what I knew of the game. Jack and I paired in playing 2014 rubbers in prison camps. It was Geoff Gregory who wrote out two pages of basic rules of 'bidding' and 'responses', which I still had and which I eventually got RM to learn. I must have been 'softer' with her than her mother for she enjoyed her return to the game. Darvall Kater, the Hallidays and Mabs Preston, our surgery sister, all joined in. Rosemarie developed into a very fine player and so got to know a lot of the older women of the district. RM was now widely accepted.

One evening we were at dinner at the Hallidays. Frank Bragg and his wife were also there. These dinners with Betty and Sep were usually great fun. With coffee and brandy came Frank's suggestion of a game of poker. He was well known for his love of this game, not only in the district but also in Sydney.

RM had never played before, while I had avoided it whenever possible. She was sitting alongside Frank, after the rules of the game had been explained to her and a few practice hands had been dealt. So the game started. RM was unsure of one hand she had so she asked Frank if he would advise her.

'Is this lot any good?' she enquired.

He sat and regarded it, in silence, for almost a minute. Then he stood up and, with his sixteen stone, lifted Rosemarie up out of her chair and shook her saying.

'How dare you. Don't you ever play this game again.'

'Hold on, what have I done?'

'What have you done! You've done something that I have never had done to me in thirty years of poker playing. You are holding a royal routine.'

Is this lot any good?

RM never has played poker since. She has always considered bridge a better game.

Mabs became so keen that we would often discuss a hand down in the surgery. We kept a pack of cards in our tea room which we sometimes used to work out a contract.

Walter who was a solo addict could not be interested in bridge, in spite of much effort on our part. Before I went to the war, when I was living with Walter and his wife Gwen, our game was 'Chinese Checkers'! It seemed to have been a pretty new game then and the three of us would spend most nights playing two hands each from dinner time to supper.

CHAPTER FIFTEEN

Exercise

Exercise was hard to come by as a busy doctor in a country town. Sleep was interrupted frequently by telephone calls, often requiring getting dressed and driving somewhere to a sickness call; mostly to a birth. Then at daylight a quick shower and a quick breakfast would usually precede the start to another busy day. Perhaps there would be a call or two before visiting the surgery or the hospital. From then on the day would be spent either in the hospital operating theatre or in the wards or the consulting room in the surgery. Movement from one place to another was always by car. The doctor could not waste time walking, even though he might have wished it. The car had to be one's constant companion. This was the pattern from Monday morning to Saturday afternoon. This sort of life excluded any real exercise. So many things mounted up during the week that Saturday afternoon, when the staff had left, and one hoped most of the population would be out seeking their own form of exercise, was a time when letters could be written and other bookwork dispatched. It was only very occasionally that the doctors would find time for sport on a Saturday afternoon.

Before the war ended and the golf course was constructed, the only outlet was at the Scone Tennis Club. Walter had long since managed to escape from this ordeal. He was a left-handed tennis player of mediocre standard but slow of movement. At the Sydney University he had established himself as a prominent golfer. In inter-varsity competitions he was feared with his handicap of two. He had warned me of the tennis club where with all the goodwill and kindness and the best cream cakes, the standard of tennis was patchy.

I was approached soon after my return by dear old Penn Richards to consider joining in for Saturday afternoon games. There were no inter-town or inter-district competitions so play was non-competitive. He put much thought into arranging the next matches on the two hardcourts. Major decisions, such as whether a mixed doubles or a ladies' or men's doubles would be played were the prerogative of Penn Richards. He was particularly keen for me to be one of his puppets. He had heard I played a bit; the club needed me.

In 1929 I won the Schoolboy Singles Championship of NSW. In 1930 I had been asked to join Jack Crawford, Harry Hopman and Jim Willard in what was the very earliest of Davis Cup practice squads. It was not known by such a high sounding name then, but looking back now, I realise that Harry Hopman's ideas of a practice squad were born then. He and Jack were good to me, the young junior with promise who was expected to be in the Davis Cup team in 1932. We met three times a week at the 'White City' and either played singles or doubles. Harry seemed to decide this question. Jim Willard had been our only representative at the Olympic Games a few years earlier when tennis was an Olympic sport. I well remember the five circles on his blazer pocket as our clothes were left on the ground alongside the court. In 1931 Viv McGrath beat me in the final of the Schoolboy Singles Championship and he joined the 'squad', while I sat for my Leaving Certificate examination and went to my father's funeral. There was no thought of lawn tennis as a career leading to security in the thirties.

The six years from 1932 to 1937 were memorable years at the university. We had many dedicated players. Each year we entered no less than seven teams in the Sydney District matches, our first team always playing in 'A' grade, with success. I was elected captain of the lawn tennis club for each of my six years, and with some effort managed to win the singles championship each of those years. My major efforts were directed to beating my examiners which I found infinitely more stressful than hitting the tennis ball. My tennis ambitions of earlier years were forcefully dismissed in order to beat these examiners—year after year. The war provided no tennis opportunities, except for that momentous 'dreamy' occasion on Timor.**

I told Penn Richards I had not played tennis for years, didn't even own a racquet. I really thought he could find someone more appropriate for his Saturday afternoon tennis club. I kept remembering Walter's warning. Penn insisted.

Being the young doctor always seeking goodwill, I went along to Shaddock's Sports Store and bought a new racquet and after a few false starts I did attend the tennis club. I did try. It was difficult. To serve without venom, to hit gently to the ladies, to make sure that I did not take too much of the play and then when an opportunity came to hit a winner down the line, to miss it was all unsatisfactory.

My form was shocking. This was helpful because my future sporadic appearances were kindly thought of as due to my poor form rather than any deeper motives on my part. The players and their spouses with the tea and cream cakes were very kind and pleasant. I was the failure.

The golf-course with its nine holes in grass greens was established by enthusiasts in the early post-war years. Water was reticulated which meant the course was usually in excellent condition. It was beautifully set among river gums on a delightful piece of flat country on the town edge.

** See 'Samurais and Circumcisions' Gillingham Printers—1985.

This was Walter's game, although it had been many years since he had addressed a ball. His clubs were old friends, all hickory shafted; the steel shafted clubs were just appearing on the market as Walter returned from England and bought the Scone practice. His desire to establish himself, apart from there being no golfcourse, meant his golf bag remained in the cellar.

My own golf clubs were inherited after my father's death in 1931. They were all hickory shafts except for the number two wood which had been a prize won by my father in some event shortly before he died. It was a steel shafted club, one of the early models which was painted a hickory colour to disguise its steel character, like all the earliest of the steel clubs.

Amongst RM's dowry, which came from Adelaide, was a handful of her mother's 'left offs'—all hickory shafted with varying degrees of bowing.

Mabs had the best set, all steel shafts with a reasonably new bag.

Sundays provided the only real opportunities for exercise for three of us. RM would sometimes visit the course during the week.

Our foursomes were fun. Walter, the only left-hander, was a tremendous hitter with his irons, not always on course, but the envy of the rest of us. His days of playing to a two handicap were only a memory, he would need fourteen or sixteen now. My own eighteen handicap had been reduced to sixteen by some pre-war mistake, hardly enough for me now. Mabs was on about twenty-four, while RM certainly needed more than her thirty-six. So our games were fun, not exhibition matches, but we did get some walking exercise, usually about every second Sunday.

Apart from the golfcourse, I never walked, except indoors or to the garage. I can only remember walking down half the distance of Kelly Street on one occasion. I never walked the length of the main street in the many years I lived there; such was the way of the doctor. I would have liked to walk more, but my car had to be my companion.

The one time that I did walk the half street in order to collect my car from Campbell's service station was memorable. I set off with 'Shadow', our black and white Cocker Spaniel, on a lead which turned out to be a mistake. At the first corner as we turned out of Phillip Street, 'Shadow' spied a cat sitting on the path outside its own home. His immediate response took me by surprise as I was more used to holding a scalpel than a dog lead. The cat, also caught by surprise, sat up stiffly against the fence and challenged him. 'Shadow' barked continuously, the cat hissed and spat and as she gave him a right hook with claws extended, she made a dash along the fence to the next corner and scuttled inside. 'Shadow' following through the half opened gate got his lead caught between the gate-post and the lower hinge. This pulled him up with a jerk, but increased his howling. He wanted to kill that cat. Miss Abbott, an aged spinster, came to the rescue of her beloved cat. She was not a patient of mine. I apologised and retreated. I would hold the lead much more firmly now.

Mrs Simmons, watering her front garden across the road, spotted me as I crossed to her side and greeted me with a large smile while I muttered something about my unruly dog and hoped she had no cats.

'No, I only have an old dog, a Fox Terrier, I have had for fifteen years'.
She wanted to talk so much that I suspected what was to come.

'Doctor, if you have a minute, I wonder if you would just have a look at mother. She fell over in the hall earlier this afternoon and I got her on to the couch in the sitting room. She seems to have hurt her hip and although she says . . . "it's nothing, don't worry about me" . . . I am concerned and was going to ring you up this evening if it was no better'.

What could a chap do?!!!

'Yes, of course Mrs Simmons. I'll have to tie my dog up. I mustn't let him go for Miss Abbott's cat again. Can I tie him to the tap here?'

I was sitting down on the couch next to the old lady when there began an awful row in the front garden. Mrs Simmons' old Fox Terrier didn't approve of 'Shadow' being on his territory and he was determined to make this clear to all. As I went out I saw that 'Shadow', being much younger was prepared for a contest, but was hampered by his short lead. Mrs Simmons retrieved her dog. I scolded mine and a separation was finally settled.

Back inside, I found what so often happens to old women when they have a relatively simple fall on to their hip. At least I thought I found she had a fractured neck of her femur which had impacted because she had been able to stagger with help, from the hallway to the sofa in the sitting room. If she had fractured her femoral neck, and it had not impacted, then she would have had no chance of moving, even with help.

I told Mrs Simmons what I suspected and said I should ring the ambulance and have her mother taken up to the hospital for a proper examination and x-rays.

My progress was slow. I hadn't gone more than 300 yards, but now I could go on.

'Shadow' led me around into Kelly Street, pulling and snorting and stopping frequently to leave his mark on selected gate-posts. It was exciting to be out walking with dad—he rarely went walking at all—he was a home dog.

As we walked past Dr Barton's house on the corner of Kelly Street, 'Shadow' found a special post which required a prolonged inspection. I waited. As I did so Mrs Lister came out from the surgery entrance. We greeted one another. I thought she was a patient of mine. In fact she had seen me only two days ago about a stomach pain which I had thought I considered properly and was in the process of investigating. She looked embarrassed.

'Oh doctor . . . how nice to see you'. After a pause, 'I suppose you are wondering why I am here. Dr Barton used to be my doctor before you came. I used to go to Dr Pye, but he didn't understand me. I know you do, but I thought I would ask Dr Barton what he thought about my pain'.

All this came out so quickly, and when she stopped for a breath I tried to put her at ease . . .

'I think you are very wise Mrs Lister. It's sometimes good to have a second opinion. Everyone is entitled to do that'.

'Oh doctor, thank you. I thought you would be upset with me, you are so understanding'.

'No, not at all Mrs Lister'.

'He did agree with what you told me. That's nice for you to know, isn't it?'

I realised the young doctor would be on trial for many years. This movement of patients from one doctor to another has always occurred, and one had to learn never to be upset by it. If you were good at your work and up to date, then it would be a one-way rather than a two-way affair.

I was wearing a white tennis hat which I now pulled down to eye level and crossed the road as we began to approach the shopping area. We had to scuttle across in more of a hurry than I was anticipating. A large red Chevrolet was being driven all too fast as it brushed past us. Walking was more dangerous than I realised. I supposed he was some traveller wanting to get on up the highway, and behind time.

We got past the park without any more than 'Shadow' exchanging a non-violent greeting with a free-roaming sheepdog-cross.

We passed Lowe's general store, a stock and station agent's and others that I had visited professionally. Theo's Niagara Cafe, the sort usually found in the main streets of most NSW towns, where a large plate of steak and eggs with chips cost the traveller two shillings, displayed several boxes of chocolates in the window. I halted 'Shadow' while I looked at these, wondering if I should go in and buy a box for RM. I decided against it, not only because I feared I would be recognised, but I was not sure what 'Shadow' might do. I hoped I would not be recognised for I felt as though I was trespassing. I became convinced the doctor should not be walking his dog along Kelly Street on a working day. I was imagining the thoughts of passers-by . . . 'why isn't he in the surgery seeing patients . . . perhaps he hasn't got many'. I was regretting my decision to walk down to get my car.

So, pulling my hat down further until I could barely see, we passed on down and around Campbell's large store on the corner of Liverpool Street on my way to their service station. We waited for the railway gates to open after a goods train had passed. We then crossed the line and reached the service station—at last.

Stewart Saunders came to me, wiping his hands on a piece of oily tow, saying my car was ready. He had nothing special to report. I had just put 'Shadow' on the front passenger's seat and was about to get in when there was a screech of brakes and that same red Chevrolet was aiming at me again. Why was he after me? Who was he anyway?

'Oh, thank God I found you doc. Teddy has been bitten by a snake'.

I asked why Mr Anderson had not taken Teddy to the surgery.

'I did. You weren't there'.

'Well, couldn't Dr Pye look at Teddy?'

'No, he's out on a country call, Sister said, so I went around to your house where your wife told me you had gone walking with the dog to get your car. That's how I found you'.

Without wasting time with further talk, I saw two bite marks on Teddy's right heel. He didn't seem too concerned. His pulse rate was up to about one hundred, but what this meant with all the excitement around him, I couldn't judge.

'How long ago was he bitten?'

'Gee, it must be nearly an hour now. He had got out of the school bus and was walking up through the paddock to the back door. That would have been some time after four. He went in and told my wife, who then had to drive out to where I was fencing to get me. Then we tore into town. It's now after five. It could be more than an hour'.

I knew nothing about snake bites. I could never remember having any lectures on the subject in our medical course. All I seemed to know was what mother had told me . . . 'put on a tourniquet, cut the area, make it bleed and suck out the blood'. Teddy's thigh already had a tourniquet round it.

Although I knew very little about the subject, I realised the sisters in the hospital would, so I ordered them straight up to the hospital. I would follow.

Off he tore up Liverpool Street, I and 'Shadow' after him. What an exciting walk we were having!!

The outcome was successful. Teddy couldn't have received much venom, for apart from slight nausea and sweating and a rapid pulse rate, he seemed to suffer nothing else. We did have an early model anti-venine, but as he was in such good condition I hesitated to use any strange serum fearing he may be sensitive. Also I seemed to have heard that the snake anti-venines we had were of doubtful value. He was quite well next day and went home.

I was convinced now that a doctor in a country town can manage his practice in a far more orderly fashion from the safety and isolation of his motor car than on foot.

Walking was not the exercise for the doctor.

CHAPTER SIXTEEN

Mixed Infections

We fell into bed long after daylight on that New Year's day of 1948. Elsie was still with us but had recently become engaged to be married. She also had got home with the dawn. We met in the kitchen around midday while RM was still asleep. I knew she would not want the eggs and bacon that Elise was preparing.

'Keep all that for tomorrow Elsie. I only need a cup of tea to take back to bed, and when madam wakes I'll get her one. I was going to wash the car but that can wait'.

I could not sleep as I began to think about my New Year's resolutions. It has always seemed to be a good time to review the past year and plan for the future. In February we had arranged to go to Sydney to see Mater for a couple of days and then go on down to Narooma to Hyland's Hotel for a week's fishing in Wagonga Inlet. We had done this early in 1947 with much success and great enjoyment. We hired a small boat with a Chapman Pup engine from Bettini's boatshed and moored it each night at the hotel's wharf. Each day the hotel kitchen would prepare a hamper but we always hoped we would add freshly caught bream or flathead to our lunch. I had earlier learnt to make a fire, let it burn down to the coals then wrap the fish, after gutting, in wet newspaper and bury them under the coals for twenty minutes. Fish steamed in this way retained more of the true flavour than cooked in any other way.

Soon after our return to practice in late February, the hottest time of the year, I was called out to Parkville, five miles north to see a sick child. It was late in the afternoon and most of us were suffering with the one hundred and four degree heat. However, none more so than Billy Sutton. He was six years old and of a family of five. He complained of a sore throat and felt sick. I found he was in fact, very sick. His pulse rate was one hundred and forty per minute, he was hot and sweaty and breathing with difficulty. He had a funny smell about him which I seemed to remember from my days at the Children's Hospital at Camperdown.

I looked down his throat. It was very red and there on his soft palate was that grey membrane which I had suspected when I noticed the smell. He had diphtheria. I suddenly realised there was no time to waste.

99

This membrane of diphtheria spreads quickly throughout the pharynx and if it should reach the larynx it blocks the airway, and causes death by respiratory obstruction.

I quickly explained the trouble to Mrs Sutton and put them both in my car and drove as fast as I could back to Scone. I rushed him straight into the operating theatre and had the theatre sister take over the anaesthetic which I had induced, while I did a tracheotomy. This is an operation, usually done in a hurry to open into the trachea or windpipe below the vocal cords. It is done by making an incision just below the larynx (Adam's apple). The cut must open the skin and expose the cartilages of the windpipe and open the latter. I did this and found it a little more difficult than I had anticipated for the trachea seemed deeper than when one feels one's own. Anyway it was just in time. The pressure in the lungs which had built up because of the obstruction was suddenly relieved by the opening in the trachea. As a result I received an explosive gust of wind and membranous material into my face. I put into this opening what is called a tracheotomy tube, a curved metal tube with a flange which fitted over the skin of the front of the throat. Tapes then tied it around the back of the neck. This tube kept the airway to the lungs open. It required cleaning frequently to ensure its patency. Also a piece of gauze was required to be kept over it to prevent the inhalation of foreign bodies such as flies.

All this only relieved the obstruction, it did not treat the underlying cause. Diphtheria was not an uncommon disease at that time so we always had diphtheria antitoxin in the freezer. Billy was treated with large doses of this and with careful nursing he recovered. The diphtheria toxin played havoc with the heart muscle so he had to be carefully nursed and rested.

Those of us involved all required prophylactic treatment with diphtheria antitoxin in an attempt to prevent our contracting the disease. All the other children were given the appropriate injection that night and the next day I arranged with the schoolmaster to have Billy's contacts also treated. I myself, who had received the full blast in my face, had a full dose of antitoxin into my backside.

Two days later I had a morning call to a house at the lower end of Kingdon Street, one of the poorer areas of Scone, to see a sick child. The family was poor mainly because the father spent most of his wages at the pub. The children all had scabies as well as what I diagnosed as scurvy. I spent quite some time examining them all and trying to get the mother to understand what was required to treat them. I thought she should do this at home, in their own isolation, rather than admit them to hospital.

That evening as I was driving home at the end of my day I began to feel itchy. RM was in the garden when I told her about my day, starting off in the scabies household.

'Right' she said, 'off with your clothes as soon as you put the car away. Don't go in the house, leave your clothes at the back door and stay there'.

By the time I had done this RM was back with a sponge and a bucket of hot water, laced with Dettol. She squeezed the full sponge over my head and washed and sponged me all over and then led me into the bathroom where the bath was already filling. I was made to soak in more Dettoled water and my hair and scalp scrubbed thoroughly. It was then she said, 'Look at you. You've got a spotty rash all over your chest and stomach'.

'Well I'm not surprised after what you've done to me'.

No wonder I was still itchy. It was not due to my morning visit nor to the Dettol. I suddenly remembered the diphtheria antitoxin. It was an anaphylactic reaction to the injection of forty-eight hours before.

I was put to bed and Walter came around to see me. He thought the whole affair was hilarious, but agreed with the diagnosis. An antihistamine injection and a good sleep found me rash free, feeling well and thoroughly disinfected the next morning.

By mid 1948 we were in Sydney staying with mother for a few days. The secretary of the BMA at that time, John Hunter, told me as an ex-POW I had priority for obtaining a new motor car. The fact that I had a car did not alter this. General Motors had brought out a new model Buick, a large bulbous eight cylindered car which took my fancy. My order was dealt with promptly and it was shortly delivered to me in Scone. It was the first in the district because of my priority. The BMA had been very helpful as was my bank manager. My annual salary at that time was about £3000 pa and my debts on my house and the new surgery had been paid. The Buick cost £920 which required an overdraft which my solicitor, Sep Halliday, vehemently objected to, saying I was reckless. Within eighteen months when I sold it for £1 600 in favour of a Mk5 Jaguar, he changed his tune. The Buick was sold to Bill Bishop, a grazier at Bunnan, who eventually lost it when it stalled in a flooded creek crossing. The wall of water washed it away to its destruction and the chagrin of his wife who had left three new pairs of shoes in the boot.

It was not long after the Buick had been delivered to me that I began to feel 'off colour'. I had a throat complaint for a day or two with a slight fever and a bit of stiffness in my jaw. I was tender around the jaw joints and wondered what what was happening when I realised I was getting 'mumps'. Swellings were appearing in front of my ears. The parotid glands were both tender. RM was horrified.

'Didn't you have mumps as a kid? My sister and I did'.

'I can remember chicken pox, measles and scarlet fever, but I don't remember having mumps. I haven't seen any cases lately. Give Walter a ring about me'.

'Oh dear, the doctor's got mumps. Oh dear, that could be serious. I'll come around'.

I had discovered these lumps as I got up in the morning so RM caught Walter before he left home.

He was smiling smugly as he entered my bedroom.

'Now you must be careful doctor. You know what will happen if you don't rest in bed for a week at least, don't you?'

I wondered if he was fooling until I thought back and suddenly realised the one dreaded complication of mumps, especially in adult males. The testicles could be affected and impaired.

'Now you must be very careful doctor. You must rest completely—and hope', as he twisted his moustached mouth in that delightful humorous way of his. We had not yet started a family, so there was need for hope.

After RM had bedded me down and told Elsie of this new problem, she went off down town for the shopping.

Campbells was the main general store which had an excellent delicatessen section which RM frequented. As she greeted Mr Gregson, the effusive and efficient manager of this section, he replied.

'Good morning Mrs Poidevin, bad news about the doctor. I hope he gets better soon.'

MI5 had nothing on the 'grape-vine' of the Scone telephone exchange!

CHAPTER SEVENTEEN

'FINE PARTS INDEED WHO CHEATS A WOMAN'
John Gay, The Beggar's Opera

'Good morning Doctor, and how are you this morning', was Mab's greeting as I walked through our clinic, a bit late, one Wednesday morning.

'Good morning Mabs, sorry I'm late, what's doing here today?'

'Well little Harry Turner just came in a few moments before you arrived and gave Molly a message for you. She was to tell you that his mother had just gone into the 'eternity' hospital and would like you to call up and see her. She didn't think she would be long'.

'Anything else?'

'Yes, I'd like a cup of tea' from Walter, as he hurried in, cutting short an answer from Mabs.

'Good day Walt. I'm finding it hard to get a go on this morning. I had a confinement at four, and didn't get back to sleep again'.

He didn't seem to take much notice of what I was saying, being more interested in a small glass bottle he had just removed from his coat pocket. He held it up in front of us. It contained one of those flying ants which seemed to come in droves on some hot nights. We used to think they preceded rain. They had ants' bodies but also two quite large very thin wings which they seemed to shed all over the place. Apparently they were short lived, coming out from somewhere to spend a very short life, invading most dwellings and being attracted by light. It was said they lived for a quick mad mating, flying wildly around until their wings fell off, then dying, making an unholy mess for the vacuum cleaner next morning.

Walter explained why he had one in his glass bottle. He had lain awake also, last night and he had come up with this answer to the problem of Mrs Ashcroft. He had worried about this patient of his for many weeks until now, when he was excited to think he had the answer.

Her story began the summer before, almost twelve months ago.

Mrs Marjorie Ashcroft was the attractive wife of Harry Ashcroft. They were the licensees of one of the hotels in the district. She was tallish with dark curly hair, vivid blue eyes, a magnificent dimpled smile which reflected her happy personality. Each drinker got the impression she was there for him alone. Harry was regarded as a very lucky man. They had two young children, their business prospered and they were considered a happy and highly regarded couple.

This was before that night twelve months ago.

The day's work had been done, the maids were tidying the bar and the dining room while Harry and Marjorie were reading the morning paper under the standard lamp. It was a night when there was a plague of these flying ants.

Suddenly Marjorie screamed. One of those insects flew into her right ear. She jumped up, shaking her head, asking Harry to 'do something'.

'One of those creatures has flown right into my ear. I can feel it buzzing and flapping about. It's making me feel dizzy and sick. Do something'.

'Well hang on, don't panic. Let's have a look'.

Harry couldn't see far into her ear. No one could without the proper instrument. So he told her to lie down while he got a little olive oil and warmed it. He put her head on to her left side and with a teaspoon poured some warm oil into her right ear.

'Ugh! that feels awful. I can still feel it buzzing and it's beginning to ache now. Take me down to see Dr Pye'.

Mabs was there when Walter got over to the surgery, just across from his home. She had the auriscope ready and the ear syringe with the flushing fluid and kidney dish at the ready.

Marjorie was very distressed. She complained of a dreadful ringing in her ear and a headache. She kept her eyes closed to try to stop her dizziness, as she kept saying, 'Get it out, get it out quick'.

Mabs steadied her head while Walter made his examination.

'It's hard to see anything definite, the ear canal has quite a sharp angle in it and there is wax and oil there. I'll have to syringe it out'.

As he checked to make sure the nozzle of the ear syringe was firmly attached to prevent its being blown off when the plunger was depressed (such a case had recently been reported in the Medical Journal of Australia), he filled the barrel with the warmed bicarbonate solution. With the first washout quite a bit of wax came out. There was also one thin wing which obviously had been left there by the misguided insect. He showed this to Marjorie who made a grunting noise as she opened her eyes just enough to see it.

'There now, let's have another look'.

Walter still had difficulty actually seeing the eardrum because of the sharp angle in the external ear canal. Also, Marjorie was not much help. She kept complaining of pain and now sickness as Walter continued to try and visualise the whole of the canal down to the drum.

'Let's just do another syringing, can you hang on a bit longer Marjorie?'

'Yes, do anything you like but get it out. I can't stand it. Get it out please'.

Mabs looked at Walter and they exchanged glances with raised eyebrows, while Harry stood by watching all that was going on.

Walter tried again, this time pushing the plunger a bit more firmly than before. Out came a bit more wax in the returning fluid, but no insect.

'Haven't you got it yet?' asked Marjorie.

'No, I've got the wing you saw and wax but I don't think there is anything else there now'.

'I'm sure it's there, my ear is aching. I feel sick and dizzy and think I'll vomit'.

Walter beckoned to Harry and they both walked out of the treatment room while Mabs continued to comfort Marjorie.

'I can't see anything there. If there were, the syringe would have removed it', Walter explained to Harry. 'I think it must have flapped against her eardrum when it first went in. This is a very sensitive part and I can only imagine that it has injured it a bit and that's what Marjorie is suffering with at present. Also she's very frightened. I can't do anymore, except to give her a decent sedative and get you to take her home to bed. I'll call out first thing tomorrow morning'.

As Walter entered the bedroom next morning Marjorie said, 'I'm sure it's gone right inside'.

'Tell me how you really feel. Is it still paining?'

'Yes, and I have a headache all over this right side of my head. Could it have gone inside?'

'There's no chance of that Marjorie, none whatever. An insect couldn't push its way through your eardrum. How's your hearing in the right ear?'

She seemed to be able to hear in that ear, but continued to complain of pain and dizziness.

Walter used the auriscope again, but he was still not able to get a full look at the eardrum.

'What are you going to do then?' asked Marjorie.

'I think we should get you down to Doctor Studley, the ear specialist in Newcastle and let him have a look'.

Harry agreed, so off they went after Walter had rung his colleague and explained the situation. He would see her as soon as she arrived.

Dr Studley, an ear, nose and throat specialist of twenty years standing, could do very little more than Walter. He assured her he could see the whole of the external ear canal and the eardrum, all of which looked quite normal, except perhaps for a little redness. This could have been due to the insect flapping about for a short time, and of course, the syringing. Apart from this there was no injury to the eardrum.

'I think it's gone inside', insisted Marjorie.

'No chance of that. It could never get past or through the eardrum. It's probably traumatised it and so has left you with some pain and other sensations in your ear, but you must believe me, it could not have got past your eardrum'.

He gave her some soothing ear drops with a bit of local anaesthetic mixed in to try to ease her symptoms and talked of the need for aspirin.

The Ashcrofts thanked him for his prompt attention and returned to their hotel.

Walter was asked to see Marjorie again the next day. She had known Walter for several years. He had confined her of her two children and attended to all of them for their ailments so that the highest level of mutual trust and faith had been established. Dr Studley had rung Walter and they both agreed that she had been unduly upset by this incident, that all was well with her ear and all she needed was reassurance with perhaps some sedation for a few days.

'Dr Studley seemed very nice, he was kind and gentle, but he didn't do anymore than you did. He assured me my ear would be all right, but perhaps it would take a few days to settle down. Do you believe that too?'

'Yes, I'm sure he's right. A few days will cause those symptoms you have to disappear and then you'll forget all about it and be back to normal again. Anything touching your eardrum is always frightening and certainly very uncomfortable, but apart from that nothing more can happen. You must believe that Marjorie'.

'Why have I got this headache all around the right side?'

'Well, we've tried to explain everything as best we can. I'm sure that it will go away in a few days. Just be patient and keep using a bit of aspirin for the time being'.

Walter saw Harry on his way out and told him the same story. He asked Harry if Marjorie had ever had this rather exaggerated reaction to anything before. Walter had seen her through her childbirths and other problems when she always appeared to react normally and as he would expect. Harry could only remember that he was a little disturbed once before, but that was long ago. Walter thought he should ask him.

'Actually it was on our honeymoon. She was a virgin when we married and I had been very considerate with her and thought all was well, but after a couple of days I thought she was a bit funny. I didn't know what was up with her. She got a bit morose and quiet, not a bit like I expected her to be. I asked her if I had hurt her but she denied that. She was quite funny for a couple of weeks, so our honeymoon was not a screaming success. But she got over it and since then she has been the greatest fun, we get on so well and she has been so happy and coped with all the problems as they have come along. However, this episode does remind me a bit of those early honeymoon days. Let's hope she gets over it'.

Walter gave this ear problem no more thought till three weeks later when Harry made an appointment to see him.

'She's gone like she did before', Harry explained. 'She still believes that flying insect got inside her head. Says she is still sore and does not feel right. When I suggested she should see you again she almost told me she didn't believe you, or even that doctor in Newcastle. She wants to see someone in Sydney'.

'What have you noticed about her since I saw her. It must be three or four weeks now, isn't it?'

'Yes, it's nearly four weeks, and in that time she has become quite a different girl. She won't let me get near her. She tried to come and help in the bar on a couple of occasions but she couldn't do it. She wouldn't talk to the blokes like she used to, and they all wonder what's wrong. In fact they are blaming me for everything. I'm really worried now Walter. What the hell can I do now?'

'Sure, it's a problem. I wouldn't have expected Marjorie to go like this. It certainly seems to have upset her mental balance. What to do—yes? Well, I suppose there are two things we could consider. If she doesn't believe Studley or me about her ear, I could refer her to one or two specialists in Macquarie Street. Maybe they could convince her. Otherwise we could consider one of those psychiatrists who are supposed to know more about the tricks of the mind than we do. They might even consider hypnosis which I see they use sometimes to convince people. They try to probe the subconscious mind to find out what is really upsetting people. I don't know what to suggest. What do you think Harry?'

'I don't know about hypnosis and that sort of thing. I think I would favour another opinion or two from ear specialists in Macquarie Street'.

'I agree. I have no real knowledge of what psychiatrists can do, so I have no faith there. I would think we could get her to see Dr Halliday. In fact it wouldn't do any harm to have her see two specialists—not because you don't believe one, but for her sake to have a second opinion may be just enough to convince her and see her back to her normal self again'.

Marjorie consented to these arrangements. She saw Dr Halliday, who confirmed the opinions of Dr Studley and Dr Pye. She also saw Dr Davy, another eminent ear specialist. All four doctors agreed that Marjorie's problem was not a physical one of the ear but a mental one.

There was something in Marjorie's genetic make-up which happened to have been triggered off by this insect penetrating her external ear canal.

Some weeks later after all this flapdoodle of the specialsits' examinations in Sydney had been gone through, Harry consulted Walter again.

'They don't seem to have convinced her Doc. She still believes that insect got into her brain. No longer can I get into her bed, no longer do I have a crowded bar between four and six every evening, no longer do we enjoy the happy household we have had for years. What the hell can we do?'

'All that's left, as far as I can see, is to try one of these psychiatrists.

There is one in Newcastle but there are many more in Sydney. If you agree, I shall make enquiries and find, or try to find, one who may be able to help'.

'Go ahead Doc, let's know when to go'.

Walter did make enquiries and he was advised to send Marjorie to a Doctor Twister who had a reputation for helping this sort of problem.

'Lie down there Mrs Ashcroft and tell me the story from the beginning'.

Marjorie was impressed when she entered Dr Twister's rooms in North Sydney. The decor and the magazines all suggested the ultimate in medical psychology. She did lie down on the most comfortable mattress and she did outline her problem.

'Yes, but you have told me all about the insect flying into your ear and how you have been examined by many ear specialists since. That, I understand. My objective is to find out why this penetration of your external ear has so upset your mental state. Will you now answer some questions and please relax, we have all the afternoon'.

Dr Twister did spend two hours asking questions which Marjorie tried her best to answer, but wondered what they could possibly have had to do with the insect in her ear. She was very comfortable all through the interrogation, but she became so bored that at times she found her concentration wandering. She wondered if Dr Twister did this sort of thing all the time. Did he enjoy it? Was he really able to cure people?

When this long interview was over Dr Twister called in Harry, who had been sleeping in the waiting room, to explain that, so far, he had not been able to get to the bottom of the problem, but he thought he could do so, if he were given permission to examine Marjorie under hypnosis. They both felt they had come so far, they might as well go the whole way and let him use hypnosis as long as, 'You're sure it won't harm Marjorie?'

'Absolutely not. No question of harm, and every possibility that I will solve her problem'.

'Well, OK, but I'd like to be somewhere about while you do it'.

'That's fine. The procedure will be done here. Miss Snoodle, my receptionist will make you comfortable and look after you while I hypnotise your wife. Would tomorrow suit?'

Under hypnosis, on that same mattress, Dr Twister asked all sorts of questions about Marjorie's relations with her parents, her schooldays, her puberty problems, her biological throughts, in fact he covered most of the periods of her growing years. Harry waited anxiously under the care of Miss Snoodle who plied him with coffee and cake for more than two hours.

'How did you get on doctor?' enquired Harry, as Marjorie was brought out to him, looking dazed and in need of make-up.

'Well I've made some interesting observations, which when I have examined them in depth, may be most useful. I feel sure your wife will feel the same when she has time to reflect on our interviews'.

That night in the Metropole Hotel, down near the Quay where they were staying, Marjorie said . . .

'I've no idea what he said or did but I have sense enough to know that I have seen the last of that couch. I still have an earache and am still convinced that insect got into my head. Let's go home'.

When Harry came to see Walter several weeks later he was shown the reports sent to Walter by Drs Halliday, Davy and Twister. The file was almost two inches thick, Dr Twister's occupying ninety-five percent. Pages and pages of beautifully typed words, including so many of the new psychiatric language that even Walter had no chance of understanding their meaning.

'What does it all mean Doc?'

'I really haven't the faintest idea. What's more I wonder if Dr Twister has, for he has come up with no solution to Marjorie's problem'.

'Don't ask us to go to any more of those specialists in Sydney. Please give her some more thought. She still has more faith in you than anyone. On the way back in the car she was able to talk to me more about her problem than she had for quite a long time and I realised what she was saying was just that. She distrusts all the specialists, especially that Dr Twister.

'I'm glad to hear that Harry, for I think I have an idea which may help, if only she and you have faith in me'.

'That's great news Doc. What do you think you can do that you haven't already done?'

'Well, I'd rather not explain my plan to you just yet, even though I know you would not tell her if I asked that of you. It is better you just leave it to me. I have thought it out in my own way, and I feel certain I can now cure her'.

'Doing what?'

'Now don't ask questions. All I ask of you is that you let me admit Marjorie to hospital for just a couple of days. There are one or two tests I want to make and I may have to give her an anaesthetic. Would you agree to that?'

'Yes I do and I feel sure Marjorie would too'.

Walter admitted Marjorie to the Scott Memorial Hospital on a Sunday evening. On Monday he arranged for a skull x-ray, using several different views to include the right side especially. On the Tuesday the operating list showed the last case for the morning as . . . Mrs Marjorie Ashcroft— EUA (Examination under anaesthesia).

When Marjorie woke on Tuesday afternoon she found a bandage round her head, especially covering the right ear—which area was experiencing a new sort of pain. She asked the Sister what Dr Pye had done, and was told he would see her early on Wednesday. But for now she had to let the

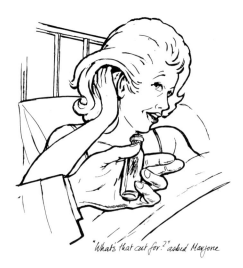

"What's that cut for?" asked Marjorie

tablets have their effect and was to sleep.

On Wednesday, when Walter had his tea in the rooms with Mabs and me, and his little glass bottle, he went off to the hospital. He greeted Marjorie with some typical remark of his, such as, 'What are you doing here. You're cured. You can go home'.

'What do you mean 'cured'? What have you done?'

He proceeded to take the large bandage off her head so he could inspect the suture line behind her right ear. It was barely a skin deep incision, about one inch long in which he had put two stitches. It was just enough of a cut to make it feel a little bit sore.

'What's that cut for?' asked Marjorie.

With that he took from his pocket the small glass bottle with the dead body of a flying insect with one wing. He was lucky that there had been another infestation of flying ants a few days earlier when he got his idea for 'curing' Marjorie.

'That insect was there, now it's in this bottle. Here, you can take it home and keep it, knowing what a rotten year it has caused you.'

Two weeks later Marjorie came to see Walter with her most grateful thanks. She knew the insect had been there. She knew he would find it. She had got back into bed with Harry again, she was back with the boys in the bar every evening, life was good again.

When Walter got home that night, Gwen, his wife said . . . 'This has just come for you.'

There was a wooden case with four dozen Melbourne Bitter beer, and a hessian bag containing two turkeys.

Women are hard to understand but I think Walter was right when he suggested there could have been a subconscious relationship between the penetration of her vagina on the honeymoon and the penetration of another long narrow canal by a flying ant. Only the GP with the advantage of a deep knowledge of his patient could reason this way.

'TO CHEAT A MAN IS EASY—BUT FINE INDEED IS HE WHO CHEATS A WOMAN.'

To salve his conscience for 'cheating', no book entry was made for that operation.

CHAPTER EIGHTEEN

The Reaper Loses

During the middle war years while I was away, many improvisations had to be made by those few general practitioners who remained to care for not only patients of their own practice, but also those of perhaps two or more other practices. The work-load on Walter for five years was heavy and constant. Holidays were out of the question.

One improvisation of which he reluctantly approved was to allow some women in an outlying area high in the ranges to be confined by an old midwife. He knew her as a reliable woman who was quite capable of conducting a normal birth and who could even handle some abnormalities, especially with telephone support. She lived in the small township of Yurli, high in the mountains many miles from Scone.

Not only was petrol severely rationed during these war years, but any form of transport was also a premium commodity. It was difficult for women during their pregnancies to make a trip of fifty miles each way to be seen by the doctor. Maybe there would be an occasional opportunity for such a visit to town but these would often depend on neighbours or other passing transport. Nothing much could be organised in advance.

The midwife was quite able to watch some of the expectant mothers through their antenatal problems which when necessary could always be discussed with Walter on the phone.

These arrangements were not ideal and not without some risk, but circumstances so often dictated the course of events. The onset of labour and the following few hours were of course the testing time for all concerned.

In the mid-winter of 1944 the isolated midwife was in trouble. The local telephone exchange mistress could not raise the Scone exchange so she tried, and got through to the exchange in another town on the other side of the ranges. She explained her problem to the doctor there.

She had delivered the baby with relative ease but shortly after the birth the mother began to bleed. The usual massaging of the uterus and the injection of pituitrin did little to stem the haemorrhage, so she was desperate to have some medical aid. She explained to the doctor that she wanted him to come out as soon as possible, at the same time explaining there would be no money in it for his services. He talked to her for a short time and advised her 'to lift the foot of the bed'. He found he could not get out!

In desperation the telephonist at last contacted Walter just as he was getting into bed after attending to a seriously ill case of pneumonia. He gave her what advice he could over the phone and said he would leave immediately and hoped the rain would not lift the creeks too much.

He arrived in the bedroom where the drama took place at 3 am. The midwife was distraught. She thanked him for coming but felt sure it was too late.

Evidence of the massive haemorrhage was there. His first look at the woman told him all. Her skin was white and cold. She was in an unconscious state, he could feel no pulse. Without wasting time to try to check her blood pressure he felt her abdomen and realised the retained placenta had been the cause of the trouble. The bleeding was reduced to a small but constant trickle, so with the minimum of preparation he inserted his hand into the womb, and with difficulty separated the placenta from the uterine wall and removed it.

His attempts to massage the uterus into a hard contraction were unsuccessful. The state of shock was extreme and the normal bodily responses could not be roused. The situation was hopeless. However he went through the usual procedure of injecting more drugs to try to contract the uterus as well as the final 'rite' of injecting adrenalin into the heart, which by now had little blood to pump.

In this situation there was no possibility of arranging for the obvious solution, namely a blood transfusion. What was possible was the injection of saline which he always carried with him, into the submammary region. He put up two saline drips into the tissues under each breast.

Again he lifted her arm and felt no pulse. The blood pressure could not be recorded.

He and the midwife gazed at each other while both experienced that dreadful realisation which was always so hard to accept. The end could not be avoided. The bedclothes were rearranged. Walter put his arm around the weeping woman and led her to the kitchen where tea was made.

He sat and listened to her tearful story of the events which led to this moment. He reassured her that she had done all that was possible—there was no blame on her management. She was not a doctor, had never even been qualified as a fully trained nurse but had experienced a bush training which over the years had helped scores of women. She would never have been expected to cope with a firmly retained placenta. Before he left, he told her he would sign the death certificate and explain all the facts to the coroner.

He had that other, always most distressing duty to do before leaving. He had to tell the husband there was little hope of a recovery.

Such was the scene Walter left as dawn was appearing and the rain had stopped. His thoughts were concerned with the tragedy. The poor husband, the guilty feelings of the midwife. Surely all this was a war casualty. These situations should never be allowed to occur in Australia after the war.

He got home to find breakfast on the sideboard, which he would enjoy after a shower.

There was something else he enjoyed far more than his breakfast. At nine, as he was about to leave for the hospital, there came a telephone call from Yulri.

'Doctor, she's alive', screamed the excited midwife.

'I don't believe it. Tell me more'.

'Well, after you left I sat crying in the kitchen with the husband, until I got control of myself and realised I had to work. I was cleaning up the floor in the bedroom when I heard a strange noise which I thought must have been my mop knocking the bed leg when it came again. It was a moaning noise. I rushed to the bed and pulled back the sheet and she moved her head. I felt her pulse and there it was, thin and fast and thready, but it was there. Imagine how I felt'.

'Yes, I can. What wonderful news. You'd better give her some more saline and fill her up with fluid as soon as she is properly conscious. Is she bleeding at all now?'

'No sign of any fresh blood at all. Her uterus is hard now too'.

'Well, for goodness sake, I'll tear up that death certificate, and get the ambulance out to bring her in straightaway'.

Drama was rarely without its humour.

DEATH CERTIFICATES, LIKE CHEQUES, SHOULD NEVER BE POST DATED.

CHAPTER NINETEEN

'Dave' at Large

The value, and even the delights of practising in a country town is that one gets to know and to watch a complete cross section of the community. In all communities there is a full spectrum of social types and customs, for example, behaviour, wealth, education, dressing, intelligence, talents and many other qualities. The country doctor sees them all, whereas the GP in the city has a more restricted view. In the cities, people are liable to sort themselves out, so that some GPs tend to attract a limited clientele. The GP in the wealthy suburb sees a vastly different social scene from the GP in the poorer suburb. One can observe many examples of this sorting out process, which is all very natural and to be expected.

Bill Small was a patient of mine in Scone. He was a heavy, rather round shouldered chap, with a small head, in his early twenties. He was on my lodge list so he often came to see me. On each visit I would usually ask him, 'What are you doing now, Bill?'

'Gee, I got a good job now, Doc. I'm helping Paddy with his carting'.

'What happened to that job you had in the butcher's shop?'

'Oh, I had to start too early there, and them knives was too sharp too. Me Mum said I ought to give it up, so I did'.

'Do you like working with Paddy'.

'We'es get on well and I like lifting them heavy parcels. Paddy says he's losing his strength, so he's glad to have me'.

So Bill could be seen sitting on the back of Paddy Curtin's dray as it moved about town. He was a simple living chap, who seemed to keep out of the brawls which often started around the pubs on pay days.

On one visit to me he wanted to ask me if he should be circumcised, as he always seemed to be 'sore there'. So we discussed this question after I had looked at his problem. During our discussion I asked if he had ever had intercourse.

'Augh gee Doc, I wish I could. I don't seem to be able to'.

'Able to what?'

'Well I tried a couple of times with two different Sheilas. I asked them, but they both laughed and told me to 'buzz off'. What 'ave I got to do Doc?'

115

'Yes, all Sheilas are different Bill, some do and some don't. Have you ever asked that young Anthea Bullock out at Satur? Some of the chaps tell me she 'pulls you on like a Wellington boot'. Did you know that?'

'I always seen her with lots of blokes. She'd be hard to get'.

'Well you'd have to work that out Bill. Perhaps if you hung around where she lives you could catch her alone some time. She doesn't seem to have a job as far as I know'.

'No, she don't work, I know that'.

It was three months later that he came to see me. Still the same area of complaint. Now he had a discharge. So I asked him when he first noticed it.

'It's about a month now Doc, and I know where I got it too'.

'Where's that Bill?'

'Well, when Paddy give me the sack, I got a job up the Rouchel helping to load some logs on to a truck. It was hot and we drank a lot of water from this bloke's tank. It tasted funny and me Mum says that's what gave me the discharge'.

'You haven't been doing any good with Anthea, have you?'

'Oh, yes, she's beaut. I did what you said and hung about her house. She likes me too—says I'm big. We have a root most days'.

'I'd better have a look at you Bill and see if it's that water you drank or whether it's anything else'.

'OK, Doc'.

He had gonorrhoea all right so I started him on some treatment. On his next visit I asked him how Anthea was.

'She's crook, she vomits a lot too'.

As I felt partly to blame I made it my business to see Bill's mother, Mrs Small. She was a lodge patient of mine. I asked her if she knew Bill was seeing a lot of Anthea.

'Oh yes, I know that. She come up to tea last night. I quite like her. I know she likes Bill too'.

'Did Anthea eat her tea?'

'No not much, said she felt sick a lot lately and gone off her munga'.

So I thought I should see Anthea's mother as well. She had noticed Anthea was not well.

'I reckon she's gone doctor. I used to get just like that everytime'.

'What do you mean by 'gone' Mrs Bullock?'

'I reckon she's in the family way'.

'Would you like me to see her?'

'I'm pretty sure she is doctor. Anyway I'll have a go at her tonight and find out. She's always around with that Bill Small. Seems a nice chap though. If she's that way I reckon they could get married. Her father will blow his gasket, but I reckon I can fix him. He'll go back to the pub. He always does'.

Anthea was pregnant and did have gonorrhoea so this might be her only chance to have a baby. This infection played havoc with the female pelvis and to get pregnant after it was always unlikely. So, as I thought this out, I realised Mrs Bullock's outlook was probably for the best, although she may not have realised it.

I began seeing Anthea regularly for her treatment and soon I was told of the impending marriage. There had been an unholy row out at Satur with Mr Bullock getting drunk and threatening all sorts of trouble for everyone—even me.

The more sensible members of this situation, Bill, Anthea and her mother were in my surgery discussing how the treatment was going and how the baby was developing. They were also discussing the honey-moon, which Mrs Bullock insisted on. She pronounced, 'Can't have a proper weddin' without a honeymoon.'

Bill suggested they should go to Newcastle, but Anthea was in favour of going to Port Macquarie, where she had never been, but had a friend who had been there and found the fishing good. I was then asked what I thought.

'Well I would suggest you go to Sydney, the biggest and best city in Australia where you'll have much more fun than in either Newcastle or Port Macquarie.'

Immediately Anthea joined in with . . .

'Well, if you go to Sydney, you'd better take Mum with you, I've been there!!'

I did enjoy country practice.

CHAPTER TWENTY

Alcoholic Opposites

Alcohol is regarded with suspicion nowadays. What a pity. A pity because I do not believe alcohol is the culprit in our society. Rather, it is the lack of discipline. Certainly its undisciplined use will lead to some sort of problem. The sensible use of alcohol is surely one of the great pleasures of life. Evidence from the dawn of history will support this view.

Alan Jones and Sid Capper, both patients of our Scone Clinic, each had his alcohol problem.

Alan was a hefty six-footer, in his mid-thirties, with ginger hair and enormous hands. He was a highly regarded horse-breaker, a one time 'gun' shearer, a fearless rodeo performer and a most useful man on any pastoral property. Alan lived in a small house in town.

Sid Capper was a wealthy owner of some very fine country. He was in his late fifties, having had a 'silver spoon' inheritance, which assured his squattocracy standing and his membership of Sydney's clubs. Sid lived several miles north of the town in a large and comfortable homestead.

Both of these characters were married with children. Alan had three, all of school age. Sid had two girls, one married in Victoria and Helen aged twenty, living at home and very eligible.

Their alcohol problems were poles apart. Both, however, were undisciplined.

Alan's beer capacity was enormous, which when tested, always led to domestic unrest. His wife and children were conditioned to this and expected it regularly on Friday nights.

Sid's capacity for spirits was just as undisciplined. He was generally regareded as a 'bottle a day' man. His blood alcohol level required topping up on waking and for his normal daily duties it required regular attention. His duties were not arduous! His wife and daughter relied on their excellent manager and staff to keep the large cheques rolling in. This pattern was the accepted norm and caused no trouble. However an occasional 'brain storm' would take over and Sid would become a 'two plus' man.

Both of these situations involved the doctor.

'It's Mrs Jones on the phone, Dear. Sounds to be quite a 'show' on there tonight.'

'Oh, it's Friday, of course. I suppose I'll have to go. I'll take it.'

'Hullo, Mrs Jones, trouble there?'

'I'm afraid so doctor. I hate calling you, but I think Johnnie's head will need stitches, it's bleeding badly.'

On the first occasion I was called to Alan's house on a Friday night I went along full of hope that I would be able to help.

The house smelt like a hotel bar and looked the subject of an earthquake. The kitchen table was on its side, the chairs were everywhere. Alan was standing, swaying widely in the midst of this theatre. My entrance seemed to steady him as he gazed groggily to get me in focus.

'Scuse me Doc, I've had a few beers and I'm not too steady.'

'Well, why don't you sit down, here have this chair', as I straightened a chair which very nearly gave way as he flopped on to it.

He seemed relieved and became so quiet, he almost slept. I was beckoned by his wife into the hallway when she told me this sort of thing often happened. She wondered if I could give him a sedative and get him quietly into bed.

I suggested we might get him to bed without a sedative but she convinced me that this had happened before when she thought he would settle down to sleep but he usually got up and started his physicals again. No, she thought I should give him something.

'Would he swallow a couple of pills, do you think?' 'Oh no', she said, 'he would never do that', she had tried that many times before—no, no, she thought an injection would be best.

I was undecided. I was quite unsure of the effect of a needle. Would he feel it if I were careful and quick, or was he anaesthetised enough to think it no more than a mosquito bite. I was frightened. However, I felt the responsibility was being put on me by his wife, and I didn't want her to think the doctor was not able to help. So I decided to prepare a sedative injection. The dosage I should use was a puzzle. Would he need a large dose because of his size, or would just a small dose be sufficient, when added to his alcoholic content? I had never had to handle this type of situation before. I was on the spot. I had to do something so I selected the dose and the sharpest needle I had in the bag and went back to the kitchen.

Alan was sitting quietly, breathing heavily, almost snoring. As I stood alongside him and lifted up his large forearm I thought he must have been asleep for he took no notice of my handling him. Again I wondered whether he should be disturbed by a needle or whether I could not use, what I thought was my better judgement and try to coax him to bed with persuasion. His wife, and by now his three sons were watching the scene. I still felt I was under trial and would be shirking my responsibility if I did not give the injection.

119

So I gently eased up his short flannel sleeve to expose the back part of his arm. I put my hand around it and realised how tough the skin was. Should I proceed or not? He was very quiet, apparently oblivious of the impending attack on his person. I felt I had control of the situation and that his respect for, and faith in the Doc would assure peace. No force was being exerted as I manipulated his arm and stood alongside him with the syringe poised. His head had fallen forward, his breathing was heavy and noisy. I would squeeze a fold of skin and quickly inject the sedative.

The skin was tough, and I was not.

Immediately he jumped up and flung his arm around, knocked me to the floor, under the overturned table, swore at his wife and kids, all the time with my needle and syringe hanging from his arm. None of the sedative had been injected. I had gained nothing—and lost my syringe. I wondered why I had been so keen to go and help. I felt this rather undignified position should not be accepted too long so I got to my feet and quickly left the scene. He pulled the needle and syringe from his arm and threw it at me as he screamed and shouted, making it quite clear that if I did not disappear I would suffer. There was no bravery in me so I wished Mrs Jones 'goodnight' and left, saying that I would ring Sergeant Bedingfield for her.

That first visit was a failure. I feared our next meeting. It was not a complete disaster however, for I saw Alan a few days later and he was his usual gentle self. He apologised if he had been rude or upset me last Friday night. We enjoyed our usual mutual goodwill and respect. Why he didn't sock me for attempting to take advantage of him only the mysteries of alcohol could understand.

On this later occasion when I was summoned to attend to Johnnie's split scalp I asked Sergeant Bedingfield to come with me. He, or his constable, or both were just as much a part of my subsequent visits as my little black bag.

Such was the effect of undisciplined alcoholic intake on Alan.

Sid's excesses were ever so different. His wife and attractive daughter were never subjected to physical assaults.

Sid needed, and lived with his 'bottle a day' of whisky. He appeared socially quite normal on this dose, though the fragrance of the flowers was constantly under challenge.

Every now and again, at about three month intervals, something happened to Sid which made him greatly increase his intake of whisky. The first signs of this could easily be recognised by his searching out the manager and picking on his ability, or lack of it, concerning some aspect of his management of the property. In between these attacks on the manager he would hardly speak to him but when the 'storm' came on he would be abusive, making wild accusations and usually ending by giving him the sack. The manager became used to these performances, put up with them, and got on with the job.

Sid's next move was to begin inspecting the books, interfere with the mail, write rude letters, begin to draw cheques and generally upset the otherwise smooth running of the estate. These signs were all too obvious. They were well known and easily detected by his wife and daughter. It was most embarrassing for them because all the town could quickly hear that Sid was having another 'turn', if precautions failed.

The usual drill was for Mrs Capper to contact Sister Flanagan, now retired from her hospital duties, who had a small cottage in the town and who would always accept Sid for the duration of these 'turns'. For some strange and unknown reason she was the only person who could calm him down and control him. Once he got there he seemed a different person, would cause no trouble, and accept her management which consisted of controlling his whisky intake and getting him back on his food. This ability of hers was magical and not easily understood. It was a satisfactory situation. The wife and daughter and the manager then had a peaceful existence, often for three or four weeks, before he would return home. There was of course, a catch in all this.

The difficulty, once the onset of a 'turn' was detected, was to convince Sid that it was time for him to visit Sister Flanagan. This was always the trouble spot and the time for the introduction of the doctor.

Now Dr Pye was the family doctor. He was always the essence of tact. His visit to the property was done discreetly, the telephone girls were never aware of these occasions for messages came personally. He was required because Sid respected him and would accept his advice to visit Sister Flanagan. He would not accept this advice from anyone else. As long as Dr Pye came to see him and had a talk then he would agree to go to town. More magic!

These arrangements worked quite smoothly. The detection of the first signs, the call to Dr Pye, the decision to visit Sister Flanagan and her ready acceptance of Sid to the room which was always kept for him, was the usual order. The system worked—mostly. There was one flaw which upset it.

When Sid's 'turn' coincided with Dr Pye's absence, I was introduced to the system.

When this happened Mrs Capper came personally to see me. She felt it necessary to explain the situation to me, face to face. She did not know whether Walter had ever mentioned the Cappers' problem to his partner. It was all most embarrassing. I had to admit that I knew only a little because Walter was very discreet and correct concerning professional knowledge and relationships.

'Of course I'll come out Mrs Capper. What time would you like me and what sort of approach should I make to Sid?'

When I entered the large white sitting room, with white carpets, white walls, off-white curtains with gold stripes and white upholstered chairs,

Sid suddenly stopped his parading and stared at me. We had met several times earlier, but through a lower alcoholic level than today. He stood for quite a time without moving, then said . . . 'Where's Dr Pye?'

'He's away. I'm his partner and have come to talk to you and help you if you'll let me'.

With that he lurched towards me so I grabbed him firmly around the chest and restricted his arms. Although I was small I found I could easily handle him. He had very little strength. I managed to push him on to the couch and sat down alongside him.

'I'll only talk to Dr Pye, where is he?'

'He's in Sydney and will be away two weeks'.

With that he struggled up and began to push me around again. He kicked but was easy to restrain.

'What about coming into Sister Flanagan's?' I asked him.

'Not until I see Dr Pye', he insisted.

As we continued to lurch about the room Mrs Capper came up and whispered to me that . . .

'It's no good doctor, you'll have to put him out'.

'How do you mean? You didn't warn me of this when I asked you what I should do'.

'When he's like this, sometimes even with Walter, a handerkerchief, wet with chloroform gets him to sleep and then we take him in'.

'What about an injection, it would be safer?' (Chloroform could be lethal if used carelessly, I didn't want to kill him and have a court case over this chap.)

'No, Walter has tried that, it makes him more difficult. Try chloro-form—as I say'.

Against my better judgment I went to my bag and put some chloroform on a piece of rag. To my surprise as I approached Sid he recognised the smell and seemed to welcome it. He was on the couch where I had put him. He grabbed the rag and began to inhale deeply. I was really surprised. I had expected a tussle.

Mrs Capper said . . . 'Now don't let him have too much or we'll never get him to the car'.

Helen had brought the Rolls Royce to the front door and as Sid slowly came out of his chloroform reverie he was quite cooperative and willingly got up. With help each side it was easy to get him into the car.

And so Sister Flanagan, with her magic, weaned him out of yet another dipsomaniac episode, back to his 'bottle a day' and normality.

Both these men had an alcohol problem, of that there can be no argument. Yet equally unquestionably, they both had a discipline problem. If Alan Jones had been a disciplined man he would have controlled his beer intake on Friday nights thus relieving his household of the weekly disturbance. In the same way, if Sid Capper had the character to discipline his behaviour, his family would have been saved embarrassment. His problem would require a greater discipline than Alan's would, for he was a dipsomaniac. In years to come 'Alcoholics Anonymous' would be available to help these ill-understood sufferers control their problem.

I guess the whole world needs discipline . . . If you haven't got it . . . you're in trouble.

CHAPTER TWENTY-ONE

The First Born

'Is your wife pregnant?' Mrs payne always asked direct questions. I liked her and respected her strong character and especially her work as president of the CWA, Upper Hunter, but I had not forgotten the 'Baby Show' affair. Was this another trap? If it were I couldn't detect its significance. These intelligent women always bothered me.

'No', was my equally direct reply.

The occasion was a Saturday afternoon at a polo carnival not far from the Payne's property-'Waverley'. Winnie and I did a lot of talking when we met at similar types of crowded functions. She had strong views on many things, mine rarely matched. It was a beautiful sunny day in pretty hilly country, on this luscious green flat turf. We should have been more interested in the thundering hooves of the polo ponies as they rushed past us but Rosemarie, as she was walking across to us, was of more interest to both of us. She had her hair cropped short. She looked attractive with a blue skirt and a matching jumper outlining her most admired figure.

'Does she look pregnant?', was my question to Winnie, as RM joined us.

'No, that's not why I asked. I just think it's time you two had some children. You've been married two years now, that's long enough. You've been getting babies for lots of other girls all around the district. It's time you had your own responsibilities'.

'It seems to me that you two are talking about me'.

'No darling, not about you, about us. Winnie is being her usual direct self and has been telling me it's time we had children'.

RM smiled sweetly, as she looked at us both, but said nothing.

'Maybe we can't; remember I was a Japanese POW. It was widely believed that lots of us would be infertile'.

'Have you tried?', Winnie insisted.

'You're probably quite right, Winnie, in your thoughts. I really think RM and I have been feeling much the same way just lately. As she was just twenty-one when we married, I did agree with her wishes to have a few years on our own, without children. Maybe soon we'll think about this again'.

'I hope so', said Mrs Payne.

We did discuss this question and we did decide to start a family. Making the decision was easy. Waiting for the pregnancy was more difficult. We were disappointed, month after month, for quite some time, so I hoped to avoid Winnie Payne as much as possible.

When next in Sydney I did have my own fertility investigated for I was not sure about our POW discussions on this subject, even though I always rubbished the possibility of future infertility when I was consulted about it in those days. There seemed to be no problem, so we just let the question ride.

One evening in the early winter of 1948, when I came in from a cold wet drive from ten miles out, I went straight up our long hallway to the sitting room where I knew there would be a welcoming fire. RM was standing with her back to the fireplace with her skirt lifted slightly, as was her habit, 'just to warm up a bit quicker', she would say. The sherry decanter was nearby with two empty glasses. She kissed me and made me almost get in the fireplace when she felt my cold hands, and then poured two glasses of dry sherry.

'Drink that and make a wish'.

'Why a wish?' I asked. 'Silly, don't you know'?

'Know what?', I was always slow on the uptake. 'Oh' as it began to dawn on me, 'you don't mean . . '.

'Yes, silly, I'm sure now'.

And so it was, we were to have a baby.

As young (RM anyway) future parents we were excited, no doubt like all with their first babies. To me, as a doctor, my thoughts were dominated by the medical aspects. RM's on the other hand, would have been far more concerned with the infinite problems of motherhood. Men, I am sure, don't think nearly as deeply as women on these occasions. Why should they, or more sensibly, how could they?'

Looking back, as far as that is possible today, I can only remember being excited. I would be a father. Winnie Payne would now be satisfied. I was not infertile. How would the pregnancy go? Who would look after RM? Walter, of course. She would have her baby here in Scone. Would all go well?

I have no doubt RM's thoughts bypassed these simple matters, and went to the much higher plane of future motherhood. How would she cope with the baby? She would be on twenty-four hour call, the man would get away to his work, she couldn't. How would this alter her life? Would she be a good mother? Would it affect our own feelings for one another? She was eleven years younger than I, but as a female, infinitely older in wisdom.

Walter, naturally enough, kept a close eye on Rosemarie. She did feel a bit 'off' in the early days but nothing requiring more than a simple gastric sedative mixture. Like most women, the hormonal changes of pregnancy agreed with her. Her friends said how well and pretty she looked. Pregnancy, in the healthy, always did this.

No one told me how well I looked, probaby because I didn't. The wet and cold weather and the full creeks on country calls gave me a worried look! However, it was also the year of the Buick. My large new eight cylindered Buick cheered me up. It coped with the creeks better than the A/40. Our Vauxhall coupe had now been sold to a local friend who always had a 'yen' for it.

Our lives did alter, mine particularly. I had corned beef and carrots for lunch and dinner every day for months. Grapefruit in sufficient numbers could not be supplied by the locals so I had to import them from Newcastle. These two most extraordinary changes in Rosemarie's eating desires were only outdone by her desire for chewing gum, which she normally loathed in any form. The cupbaords were stocked with these unusual items. Poor Elsie, gone were the days of normal roast dinners. It was now two grapefruit for breakfast—corned beef and carrots for the rest of the day, with PK in a large dish on the sideboard. We gave up entertaining.

Other peculiarities arose. A man is not a man until he has lived through his wife's pregnancy. He must live with it and keep his senses alert. He will be much wiser, but more confused in his attempts to understand the female mind. What a maze! One might think that a doctor, whose main efforts were in midwifery, would have an advantage over other males. This is not true. No male, professional or artesan, can understand the pregnant mind.

Research workers today pontificate at great length on their expertise but they are still 'babes in the wood'. Those placental hormones may be measured by the experts but their effect on the mind is a mystery. Each hormone may be measured to a millionth part of one per cent with confidence but will that explain why someone, who detested the use of chewing gum, even by others, suddenly become addicted? The rearranging of the sitting room furniture, with the exclusion of the male's favourite 'poof' may be ascribed to the 'nesting' influence, but it cannot be resisted or objected to without running the risk of a confrontation, even to the extent of tears. That really is an interesting subject. Why are tears more plentiful during pregnancy?—the experts can't explain that— so like many other things that they cannot explain, they pretend they don't exist. All may be going well with a particular conversation when suddenly the 'little woman' will be in tears, without reason.

Do the placental hormones take responsibility for the dislike of her favourite perfume and its replacement with one that was previously considered 'in poor taste?'

The getting up at two am to visit the bathroom can confidently be explained by the knowledgeable doctor as due to pressure on the bladder by the baby. Can his knowledge explain why our prospective mother will continue sitting there for a further hour reading an Edgar Wallace, an author previously shunned?

Why should a woman who adored playing bridge find that it had no interest for her while in the pregnant state only to recover her enthusiasm after the pregnancy?

Why should a woman only experience satisfactory orgasms when she is pregnant? I had such a patient who had consulted me complaining that in her early days of marriage she thought she had experienced an occasional orgasm. She had thought that sexual intercourse was pleasant. This was until some years later when she got pregnant, she experienced what she interpreted as the fullest orgasms. These were much stronger and lasted so much longer than any she thought she might have experienced earlier. All this became quite a problem for her husband. Not only was she always wanting sexual intercourse, she was always wanting to be pregnant.

The understanding of the female orgasm is as mysterious as the universe. This case, just quoted, suggests that there is some hormonal association; a very strong suggestion; yet try as we may with hormonal therapy in the non-orgasmic woman, we fail. There is a much greater depth required to understand the female orgasm than a knowledge of hormones.

One of my patients always knew when she was pregnant because she developed three small pimples on the left side of her nose within a week of her missed period. They would remain there until six weeks after the delivery of the baby. This woman had five children, each time with the three pimples. She was fascinated, but not worried, for there was a cosmetic disguise for them. The several dermatologists in Sydney, whom I asked to see this patient, had no idea as to their cause. One wisely said they were due to the pregnancy hormones! He was ahead of his colleagues. The oldest and cleverest specialist of the lot (and cunningest) asked if my patient had these three pimples before and when she admitted this he said 'well my dear you've got them again'.

The skin problems of pregnancy are a complete mystery to the skin specialists. Because they cannot handle them except by substituting the modern cortisone cream for the calamine lotion of the forties, they really show very little interest in them. At least they now recognise the fact that the so called 'stretch marks' are not caused by stretch but by steroidal changes induced in pregnancy. It took an obstetrician's research work to prove this.

No, the pregnant woman, with her own peculiar abberations, is no easier to understand than why two birds, who don't see each other for most of the year, will fly 10000 miles to mate, with no other, on a remote island in Antarctica.

One night, in late 1948, when RM had quite a sizable abdomen, I arrived home after a midnight call to 'Brancaster' to find her sleeping heavily. I got into my bed quietly and without disturbing her sleeping rhythm. As I was lying awake, waiting for sleep, I was thinking of the happiness the newest mother in Scone must be enjoying with her new baby alongside her, when I heard a strange clicking noise which I thought came from outside the bedroom window. It was a sharp 'click,click'. I couldn't make it out, when it happened again. There must be a prowler there. I got up and in dressing gown and slippers went out the back door and around to the bedroom window. I went carefully and very bravely for I didn't know what I should meet. I eventually got right up to the window, finding nothing suspicious, when I heard—'click, click'—again. It now seemed to be coming from inside the window. I was puzzled. Back to bed wondering if RM was not really asleep and 'pulling my leg' by playing one of those toy frogs we used to squeeze to make this noise. This would be quite unlike RM who really liked her sleep. I crept up close to her face. She seemd to be sound asleep. I made some whispering noises close to her but she didn't respond. I was sure she was soundly sleeping.

Back to bed and as I waited for more of these clicks, trying to work out what was going on, I fell asleep.

When I woke it was daylight and RM was awake. I told her of my experience. She had been asleep and heard nothing. But she said, 'It's funny you should mention this because for the last two or three days I have thought I heard clicking noises but could not find out where they came from. I would have told you only I felt so stupid; thought I must have been imagining things'.

'Well it tricked me last night. I don't understand it. But I must be up. I'm late now'.

That evening RM told me she had heard the clicks again while she was

128

reading on the sofa during the afternoon. She said she was sure they were inside her!!

'What rot. There's nothing inside you that could make that noise'.

'Well you'll see. When we are reading in bed tonight, it might happen again. I'm sure it's the baby'.

There was no doubt of it. I could even 'feel' the clicks as I was able to feel the baby. It was an active foetus. RM had commented on this many times. It always seemed to be rolling around, kicking her book about as she rested it on her tummy while reading, but these clicks were something new. My experience of pregnancies was of course, relatively small, only a very few years, Walter's was longer. I told him about it. He thought I was joking.

We were both intrigued. We had both agreed with RM—the noises were intra-uterine. There was nothing in the books about this. The only noises attributed to intra-uterine life, mentioned in the texts, were 'foetal cries'. For many years these had been heard and reported and recorded now in text books. Occasionally, for some reason, the foetus was able to make an 'intra-uterine cry'. There seemed no doubt of this, in spite of its rarity. There was no mention of 'clicks' anywhere. We could only think they were associated in some way with either a joint movement (we oldies have clicking joints) or had something to do with the 'vernix caseosa'—that is, the sticky pasty sort of secretion that seems quite excessive on some babies. This vernix sometimes covered the whole baby at birth and was like a thick creamy cheese. It was supposed to be very nourishing and when fed to experimental tadpoles made them grow twice as fast as the controls. All very exciting, but could two surfaces covered in this, cause clicking when separated?

It was all just another mystery for when Prue was born she gave no explanation of what she had been doing to confuse us. This was all true—a complete mystery.

There is no doubt—man must live through a pregnancy in his own house. The young unmarried doctor, looking after pregnant patients at their antenatal visits, could not be blamed for having little conception of the pregnancy experiences of his patients. He saw them once a month, more frequently in the later months, he took their blood pressure, tested their urine and felt the baby. He knew and saw nothing of the really interesting and extraordinary happenings unless and until he lived with them.

RM was always a delight to me but she was 'different' during her pregnancies. Even now, she admits this but also admits that the husband could probably notice more of this than she herself.

She really had a good pregnancy, until the end. She would not come into labour. We were sure of the dates. She was due early in February. I had taken her down to the surgery one Sunday morning in mid-January to take an x-ray of the baby. It was past the thirty-sixth week because the femoral epiphysis was well developed, a certain landmark. She should have the baby early in February. To my horror I also found the baby to be settling into the pelvic brim as a breech presentation. This, we did not want. I was able, with luck and very little effort, to turn the baby so that its head presented.

Walter and I (and RM) waited daily for some activity. When she was a week overdue we agreed she should take some quinine tablets, which was a recognised way of starting contractions. The result was most unpleasant for RM. She quickly developed ringing in the ears and a succession of rigors. This shouldn't happen (I have often thought she had her wires crossed). After all this, no contractions. What did develop was a craving for a roast dinner. Elsie was delighted. Castor oil was next suggested but completely rejected by RM.

After two weeks Walter and I were nervous wrecks. Why wouldn't she come into labour. She jumped off the kitchen table, I took her for long walks at night. She had to carry the load; I couldn't help. Neither did the walks. RM got the brilliant idea of having a round of golf, plenty of swings with the driver. This did the trick. At last I was able to take her around to 'Brancaster' and notify Walter.

That night of 24 February, 1949 was long and sleepless for RM, also for Walter and me.

Sister Batterham had gone, Sister Tuite was now in charge. She attended to Rosemarie during her tedious sleepless night. Walter was there, in and out many times, always returning to me. I remained in my sitting room with the fan and the coffee service. Progress was slow, Walter was worried and we broke RM's beautiful coffee pot. We were never sure who did it. A tense night indeed. Even our Cocker Spaniel appreciated the ordeal with an occasional long low howl.

It was ten-thirty on the morning of the 25th before it ended. Rosemarie suffered most, I next, Walter after that, then Prue, our first born, comfortably holding the secret of the 'clicks!'

And so our world changed. RM was now a mother, a very tired one, and one well prepared to face her new responsibilities. I was a father who had learnt a lot about the lifestyle of a pregnant woman and therefore probably a better obstetrician. Prue only cared about her comfort and her next feed. Our lives would change.

CHAPTER TWENTY-TWO

Climbing the Specialist Ladder

For some time now I had decided that I would specialise in Obstetrics and Gynaecology. The Council of the Royal College in England decided to help those colonials, who wished to become members of this august body, by holding a full examination in Australia. There were many of us who had lost so much time from our profession because of our involvement in the war years, who now found it dificult or impossible to afford another year or two in England. The examination would be held in Australia in September and October 1950.

My application as a candidate would be accepted if I were to do a six months period in residence at the Royal Hospital for Women, Paddington. Although I had spent two years in residence at Royal Prince Alfred Hospital after graduation, I had done no residence in a women's hospital. This was essential before I would be allowed to sit. At the time I thought this rather stern but I accepted it and arranged to do my six months from April to September 1949. Walter agreed, and I was to provide a salary for a locum tenens. Walter could decide whether he needed one or not.

RM had a Tresillian mothercraft nurse for the early part of my absence in Sydney. I had the Buick which got me back to Scone about every second weekend. Prue progressed normally, while RM remained thin and looked tired. She had a miserable six months.

Another requisite for my candidature was the conducting and recording in detail, of twenty complicated obstetric cases and ten gynaecological cases. It would have been difficult to gather these in Scone, in any case, so my residency in Royal Hospital for Women was essential. It was a busy six months. The drive up and down to Scone could rarely be done in under six hours, the roads were narrow, right up the coast to Newcastle, and often heavy with traffic. I usually timed my exits from Sydney after work on Friday, which meant a midnight arrival in Scone. Many times I would drive into the garage and go into the house to find RM curled up asleep in her armchair, book on lap, in front of the dying fire. That winter was cold and wet. There were no heaters in cars then, so an overcoat and gloves were needed; any heat from the engine being quite inadequate for comfort.

RM put up with a lot that year. Elsie had left to get married and Eunice had to be trained. The Tresillian nurse stayed only for six weeks and I was away for six months. However it was a period which we hoped would pay off in the long run—if I passed.

RM had also put up with quite a lot in 1948 during her pregnancy months, because of my desire to play in the lawn tennis singles championship at my club in Rose Bay. The Royal Sydney Golf Club held the tennis championships during the winter months. There were several beautifully kept grass tennis courts behind the large hedge inside the fence on to New South Head Road. I had played very little tennis there. On my visits to Sydney I did play quite a bit of golf and sometimes a game of squash. Anyway, as I had never entered in these tennis championships previously, I selfishly or otherwise, decided to enter for the singles. There would be about six rounds to the finals, one round to be played each weekend. After my win in the first round I approached the secretary to ask if in the event of my winning the next round, it would be possible to play two rounds the next weekend. This, I was told, was out of the question. The rules must stand. No exceptions could be made. This meant a four-hundred mile drive down and back each weekend for one round.

I was very determined to win so I prepared for six weekend trips to Sydney. I prayed for fine weather each weekend otherwise rain would mean another four-hundred miles.

Rosemarie's patience, the Buick's tyres and my opponents all suffered. I won the singles that year—1948—beating Reg Bowman in the finals, so my name appears on one board in the clubhouse. I knew it would never appear on a golf board, unless it were a 'flukey' hole-in-one. It doesn't appear!

Of the twenty complicated obstetric cases, which I was required to conduct and write up, I kept room for one unusual case which I had at 'Brancaster'. I wanted to put this one in my book, which had to be sent to the examiners in London, because it was such a rare case. There was very little reference to this sort of case in some textbooks and none in others.

It was a case of a 'blighted twin'. Sometimes in a twin pregnancy one twin dies, at the expense of the other. This, in itself, is not so rare, the dead twin being born with the live one, at the time of labour. In fact there are many different possible outcomes with one foetus dying in a multiple pregnancy. My case was so rare because the dead twin had died when they were about eighteen weeks developed. The live one proceeded normally and as it grew it squashed its dead mate against the uterine wall so firmly that it finished up as a flattened curved plate of dead tissue. When the normal baby had been born, which was quite uneventful, this flattened object came out with the after-birth. It was about eight inches long, curved and flat and grey in colour. I had never seen this before, even at the Royal Hospital for Women, in my six months there, so I decided it was worthy of a place in my book. This object, the flattened dead twin, was properly called a 'papyraceous foetus'.

The other unusual feature of this case, something the examiners would never know, was that it was washed along the gutter in Kelly Street, Scone after a heavy rain storm. I needed petrol in my car. It was still raining as I pulled up at Firth's garage with the driver's side alongside the pump. As I got out quickly in the rain I kicked the glass jar with my papyraceous foetus in formalin, so that it fell on to the asphalt, the jar broke and the foetus was washed down in the gutter. There was a drain not far away so that I had to run hard and recover it from the gutter before I would have lost it forever. Why was it under my feet in the car?— I had just been to the 'Advocate' office where Jack Smith had taken several photographs of my specimen for my book.

So that big Buick had a very busy two years on the road up and down to Sydney apart from many other trips before I sold it to Bill Bishop at Bunnan. It was then, early in 1950, that I got the best car I ever owned—the black 3½ litre Mark V Jaguar.

Prue was not unlike most other babies, in that somewhere along the line, mothers had to cope with various feeding problems. Prue fed well in the early months, put on lots of weight and gave no trouble. After the first lower incisors appeared, and spoon feeding of soft foods was begun, she developed the annoying habit of allowing her mouth to be filled, then instead of swallowing it, she would blow it back into Rosemarie's face. One Saturday morning, after my return the night before from Sydney, I watched RM preparing to feed Prue. The nursery was large, had all been newly painted and prepared before Prue arrived, and had a polished board floor with mats. The high chair was now in the centre of the room with Prue in it and her feeder in place. In the Beatrix Potter bowl was grated apple. RM with a macintosh, buttoned to the throat, and a waterproof golf hat, sat opposite the little horror as the feeding was about to begin.

The first couple of mouthfuls went down normally. Whether Prue thought that was sufficient or whether it was time for the game to begin, who knew. The third mouthful went in, then the delay, then the explosion. Apple dripped from RM's eyebrows. Prue was convulsed with laughter.

'Here, you take over'.

This novelty startled Prue. Dad had never done this before. The next two mouthfuls went down normally.

'You see, she just wanted a change'.

'You wait'.

Sure enough, the game began again. Why do some children think up these games?

.. sure enough the game began again !

This trauma for RM went on regularly at feeding times. RM had been advised (not by me) to be patient. It was said that Prue, in time, would drop the habit and feeding could then be done without the macintosh. Her adviser insisted that under no circumstances was a scolding permitted. Psychiatric teaching had made it quite clear that lifting a hand to a child was unpardonable—what rot!!! The wooden spoon had been the way all previous generations had been disciplined; who were these psychiatrists who thought they knew better?

Rosemarie, as a new mother, was trying to conform to these teachings, and did for quite a few days until her patience was exhausted and her natural response took over. Prue was soundly spanked, completely disrupting the feed. Back to the cot she was put, howling, fit to kill.

'I don't care if I did hurt you', screamed RM as she slammed the nursery door.

Prue never spat her food back again. She had learnt her lesson the proper way.

My six months at Royal Hospital for Women was interrupted by lobar pneumonia. I thought I felt sick as I drove home one weekend. The next two weeks I spent in bed at home awaiting the crisis, which came about the tenth day. Walter visited me two or three times a day. As I was convalescing we talked a lot and it was then we discussed taking in a third partner. Our practice was growing and our net incomes indicated that we would be able to take in a third man.

Following our announcement we had several enquiries. Those candidates we thought suitable were invited up to Scone for an interview and to let them see what we had to offer. The intending partner would usually drive to Scone, sometimes with his wife. Walter and Gwen would accommodate them. We would all have dinner together after which the girls would go to the sitting room, Walter and I, with the applicant, to the den. Several came. Walter and I usually agreed, we knew what we wanted. Some eliminated themselves in the first few moments, for multiple reasons. We found our first impressions were usually correct.

It was during this selection time that I noticed for the first time, a trend which I did not like, and one which was to develop into horrendous proportions in the future and eventually change the face of medicine.

The major questions which most of our applicants were so keen to concentrate upon were twofold. Firstly, what would be their guaranteed income and secondly what time off would they get?

At the time, although the emphasis on these questions grated on me a bit, I did not realise that this was the beginning of commercialised medicine. Walter and I, and our fathers before us, would never have put much importance on these questions. We worked in medical practice because we had that desire. Our rewards were the helping of the sick and the goodwill of the community. Income was not of major concern, neither was time.

Looking back now, it seems certain that the 1950s saw the beginning of the decline of the medical profession.

We had trouble selecting a third partner and in the end, probably with some desperation, I interviewed a young doctor in Sydney and recommended him. Walter who did see him briefly was not that impressed, but agreed with me. I think he did this as he was planning to take Gwen to England early in 1950 for a six months holiday. He had not been back since 1931 and the war years had tired him. They both really needed a long holiday away from all the cares of practice. It was I who made the mistake. My judgment was wrong. My selection, in time, proved to be neither acceptable to Walter nor me nor the people of Scone. He was short tempered, ill-mannered and rude.

Our practice and the people of Scone suffered during 1950. Walter was away and I was committed to studying for my membership examination of the RCOG, which meant an occasional trip to Sydney for lectures, which I had chosen to attend from a whole series, provided by the specialists in Sydney. I was the only candidate from the country among a field of twenty-five. The others were mostly younger doctors, graduates of the war years or later and who occupied hospital posts. They were the specialists of the future. They had all the advantages of their hospital training positions. I was regarded as somewhat of an oddity, two-hundred miles away in a country practice. Why hadn't I arranged to attend all the lectures and tutorials and been in a training post in a city hospital? What chance did I have of passing such an examination? These were my thoughts, also. Naturally I doubted my own wisdom of even continuing at all under the circumstances.

I did receive encouragement from Professor Bruce Mayes of Sydney University. He persuaded me to continue with my plan. The more that sat for the examination the better the English examiners would be pleased and the more justified would become the decision to hold the examination in Australia. Bruce was keen to see a specialist in O&G in a country area.

For the month of September 1950 I had to study most intensively which meant I had to further disrupt our practice and put in a locum. Maureen Coghlan was a delightful girl who fitted into our household and was liked by my wife and by the patients. In fact in the six weeks she was with us our patients scrambled for her attention rather than of our third partner. I shut myself in a verandah room, only emerging for meals and to discuss odd practice problems with Maureen.

I became tensed up, no doubt was difficult to live with and slept badly.

The day of the written paper arrived on 3 October, 1950 in the Great Hall of the Sydney University. I had been staying with my mother in her home in Rose Bay. I slept badly, got up early and because of the likely traffic I left there at 9 am in my Jaguar for the 10 am examination at the University. I was full of knowledge and hope. As I was driving along Cleveland Street a car came out suddenly from a side street, which made me brake and swerve quickly. In spite of this he hit my left front mudguard. We both stopped and spoke rather sternly to each other and took names and addresses. The left wheel did not seem to be affected although the mudguard required a bit of pulling away from it. I explained I was in a hurry to get to an examination and left. A few hundred yards further on I thought the steering felt different so I stopped and found the left front tyre quite flat. Bother! I would have to change the wheel, this would make my hands dirty and time was getting on. The spare wheel in the Mark V Jaguar was stored underneath the boot and was really quite difficult to get at. My hands were shaking as I wound the screw to let it down, but soon I was able to get it out. To my horror, I found it almost flat. I could never remember looking at it, ever since I bought the car nine months ago. What would I do now? I looked about and fortunately saw a petrol pump across the road in the next block so I hurriedly wheeled it down to have it pumped up. The chap was quite nice but told me the motor on his air compressor was away being repaired. Did he have a hand-pump? He thought there was one out the back. He would see. Eventually he pumped it up by hand, while I was dancing about wishing he would hurry. Time was scarce now. I left him ten shillings and wheeled it back to the car.

Where was the jack? I had never had to jack up the front of the Jaguar before. It was not an ordinary jack, a special sort which had to be inserted under the carpet and through the floor and then wound up from there. It didn't take too long to sort that out, but I found I had to let the wheel down again before I could loosen the nuts. Once I got them all loose they gave no trouble. I quickly took off the wheel, replaced the spare and tightened the nuts. I bundled the disabled wheel into the back seat, the boot was too small to take it and I didn't have time to fit it up into its proper place. It was now 9.55 am. Off I went. It was only about half-a-mile to the University now. The entrance into the grounds, in City Road, was closed. The gate had been damaged and men were repairing it. I begged them to let me in—I had an examination paper at ten and it was past that now. No: they couldn't and wouldn't let me in. I would have to go back to Grace Brothers corner and then out to the Parramatta Road entrance. I just missed the green lights and there were many cars in front of me wanting to turn into Parramatta Road. I was most agitated. I had to wait. The lights turned green—at last. The car in front of me stalled. Damn!! However, I just managed to get around him and came to the lights as they turned red again. Blast and damn!! Would I never get there.

I was first away on the green, tore up the road into the University grounds and up to the front of the Great Hall. There were only a few cars there so I had no trouble parking. I hurriedly washed my hands under the tap on the lawn just outside then rushed in. Way down the far end I saw my fellow candidates all writing away madly. The invigilator was most surprised to see me. He knew he should have had twenty-five candidates. It was now twenty minutes past ten. I had lost twenty minutes. The rules said all candidates would have to hand in their papers at 1 pm sharp—no exceptions could be made. I started with a major disadvantage.

I grabbed the paper and saw three questions. I read them all quickly because of my agitated state. The first question was to do with anuria (suppression of urine). I could answer this well enough. I had tipped it.

I put my hand in my coat to take out my pen, which I had carefully filled up earlier at home, and it was missing. Damn!!! It must have fallen out when I was changing that wretched wheel. Had the invigilator a pen he could lend me? No, he didn't have one. However he would see if some other candidate had a spare one. He walked along the rows, so slowly, I thought he was being deliberately obstructive. Some candidates had two pens but none was prepared to lend me one in case his first one ran out. Mean lot!!! No pen. I had a pencil. Could I use that? Well he didn't mind but he didn't know what the examiners would think. I would use a pencil.

I answered the anuria question fairly quickly but was still a long way behind time. The second question was to discuss the lymphatic drainage of the cervix uteri (neck of the womb). In my agitated state I had read the question in a hurry and without thinking I wrote all about the lymphtic drainage of the uterus. It was so easy to answer the wrong question if it had not been read correctly. The third question required a long answer. It was now a quarter-to-one. I would never finish. My pencil was practically blunt by now. I would do my best. The invigilator rang a bell exactly at one o'clock and told us all to stop writing. I tried to get a couple more sentences in, when he growled at me—so I had to stop. As I looked at the pencilled scrawl I realised no examiner, in his right mind, would even attempt to unravel my answers—in pencil!!! This never happened in London. Dirty fingermarks on all the pages—no, this chap should never be allowed into the august college. I was devastated. I had wasted a whole year or more. I had been quite unfair to Rosemarie and the practice. I thumped the examination desk and screamed out in fury.

It was then I woke up as my mother was knocking on my door to tell me it was breakfast time. — What a nightmare!!!

CHAPTER TWENTY-THREE

Farewell to General Practice

Like most of my dreams, throughout my life, the theme was frustration.

The actual papers on 2 and 3 October were each of three hours with three questions each. I felt that I had done well enough to pass these providing the examiners were reasonable. I returned to Scone straightaway with instructions to return two weeks later for the clinical examinations.

These were held at Crown Street Women's Hospital. Each candidate was given a patient to examine—do a complete history-taking and full examination and then await questioning by two examiners. This was my 'Achilles Heel'. My clincial experiences in the field of O&G in Scone did not match those of the other candidates from the major Sydney hospitals.

My patient had an obvious large abdominal tumour. It was in the interrogation and the discussion that I performed hopelessly. I was not sure whether I had even made the correct diagnosis and this, of course, was influencing all my subsequent answers. I almost panicked. I felt I had failed.

Next came a direct confrontation across a table with two examiners for the viva voce. Any questions could be asked. One examiner had come from England, the other from Melbourne. It was a torrid half hour, parts felt comfortable, others very much the reverse. Finally there was a course through the pathological specimens and microscopic slides of various tumours. I had spent most time on my Sydney trips studying these, so again I felt I may have passed. It was definitely the long clinical case which would flaw me. I left dejected. Most of my colleagues, in discussions afterwards, seemed satisfied with their performances. I returned to Scone.

The Bachelors and Spinsters Ball was in progress in the large hall when I got back about ten that night. RM, as one of the matrons on the organising committee, had played a large part in the decorations. I knew she would be there.

'How did you go Darling?'

'No good, I blasted my case. Let's forget it'.

'Hullo Mabs dear, you look happy, Is all going well here?'

'Sure. I must be the oldest spinster here, but I am really enjoying it all. Why don't you ask me to dance? It would make my night to dance with our brilliant young doctor'.

'I've never had a chance to dance with you before, I know I shall enjoy it, but you're not going to dance with a brilliant young doctor. I messed up my case. I'm sure it wasn't an ovarian tumour now that I look back on it, yet all my discussion assumed that it was. Those wretched examiners were clever; just kept smiling at me as they let me kill my chances. I feel so stupid. I really needed more clinical experience. Sorry about your feet, I never could dance'.

'I'm sure you've done better than you think. Anyway it's all over now. Are we going to see you back in the surgery tomorrow? So many patients are waiting to see you'.

'Sure, I'll be there at eight-thirty, to start to catch up. Thanks for the dance. Let's go and see Rosie and get some coffee. I haven't had lunch yet. I need something'.

I danced with RM and some of the hospital sisters and had a good feed. I was glad to be back in the bush. I would forget all about Sydney and the case I fumbled.

In the mail was a letter from Walter. He and Gwen would arrive back on the *Dominion Monarch* berthing in Sydney in the third week of November. RM and I would go down to meet them.

* * * * * * * * * *

It was a beautifully cool sunny morning as we watched this monster berth in Circular Quay. We got on board and found Walt and Gwen surrounded by their voyage friends. They had a good trip via Cape Town. Walt and I dropped back into our own very comfortable relationship, we always talked so freely and honestly together. He wanted to know how things were at home, how the new partner was, how I had got on in my examination and had I taken delivery of his new car and brought it down?

'Yes, it's parked almost alongside'.

'That's good. Gwen seems to have collected so much stuff I'll be able to get a lot of it straight into the car. From memory, when I ordered it, I think it has a reasonable sized boot'.

'When you've got yourselves through customs, what about lunch at the Golf Club? RM and I have some things to get in town. Would you meet us out at Rose Bay by one?'

'Great. I'll get through customs quickly. I've fixed that up already. We'll be there and look forward to it'.

By Christmas that year we had all got back to normal again in Scone, after a very disruptive year. There was no doubt that the practice suffered during 1950. Alister McMullin was the first to point this out to me directly. Before my examination he told me that several patients had spoken to him about their dissatisfaction. Alister was a very old friend of Walter's and mine. We had seen a lot of each other before the war. He had a property, 'Yarramoor', out on the Bunnan Road and was one of the respected bachelors of the district. He was later to become President of the Senate and receive a knighthood. I had suspected what he told me. The reasons were all too plain to see. Walter's absence was the main one. My absence and the presence of a third partner with an occasional locum, over a period of almost a year, certainly lost us some patients, but more importantly, the comfortable old feeling between the community and the doctors had suffered. Complaints had begun to appear that sometimes the doctor was unavailable, especially at night time. There were vague complaints that our new partner had refused to visit, especially at night times, to out of town calls. He argued that he could give advice over the phone, and even on occasions he had ordered the ambulance to go out and bring the patient in to the hospital and he would see him in the morning!!

Walter and I certainly found problems which we hastened to solve. Most of the people were happy again that we were back. However, it was made quite obvious that our third partner would not be generally accepted. Walter was their beloved; I was tolerated, but not so our third partner. Between ourselves, we realised his time in Scone was limited.

It would be unfair to put all the blame on one. No doubt we all contributed, because of our doings in 1950, to a changing attitude towards 'the doctors'. The whole social scene was beginning to change. The early post-war years brought great changes from the older ways of life. Full employment, higher wages, greater expectations with the great revival of primary industries (wool even reached 240 pence a pound) all forecast a different world. This certainly rubbed off on medical practices, not only in Scone. The old fashioned customs of the doctor always being available, always a friend of the family and always willing to do what he was asked, so often for no reward, were disappearing. Every year, since I went to Scone in 1939, our bad debts were rarely less than 20 per cent which we would write off each year, much to the disapproval of our accountant.

On 23 February 1951 I called in at the surgery to be greeted by Mabs . . . 'Good morning doctor and how are you this morning?'

'Better than I was this day nine years ago.'

'How do you mean, what do you remember then?'

'How could I forget, you mean. It was this day in 1942 that I became a POW of the Japanese. How do you think I feel today? I am free, I'll laugh all day. Where's the mail?'

There was one letter which was short and to the point. It interested me and would alter my life . . .

'Dear Sir,

I am pleased to inform you that at a meeting of council held today you were elected to membership of the college!'

I really had forgotten about the examination results. We had all been told we would not receive the results for a considerable time. All the papers were to be sent to London for marking and then there was to be a combined meeting of all examiners. It would probably be three months before we would hear anything. I didn't care really. I knew I had failed and anyway I was back in practice with plenty of problems and interests. The result, either way, would not mean much to me. Then this letter came . . .I could have been knocked over with a feather. I took it out to show Mabs. She hugged me, kissed me on my cheek and said, 'Go and ring Rosie at once'.

RM had always been sure I would pass. She was pleased and excited but retained her calm and confident self. What a fluke!! I wondered if they let me through simply because of my efforts at sitting for the examination from a country practice; but this would be most unlike the English! I considered I was lucky especially when I learnt later that eight of our twenty-five had failed. Shortly afterwards an invitation arrived.

The conferring of the diplomas would take place in the Great Hall of the University and would be followed by social events over a three day period. Sir William Gilliatt, the President of the RCOG would come out from England to conduct the ceremony. All wives were invited; it would be a great occasion for Rosemarie and me—to meet all these important people.

Something else happened at one of the social events which was to change our lives. I received a verbal invitation, from a senior gynaecologist from Adelaide, to consider accepting a new appointment, just about to be advertised, that of the first Medical Superintendent of the Queen Victoria Maternity Hospital.

'But I'm quite settled and happy in my practice in Scone and really have no intention of moving. Thank you for asking me but really I don't think I'm interested. Anyway, I don't think my wife would want to move'.

'Well I've just met her, I know she's from Adelaide. I know her mother well and often see her at the golf club'.

'I don't think Rosemarie wants to return to Adelaide, she's very happy and has lots of friends in Scone. She loves the country'.

'Talk it over with her. Think about it. It might be worth coming down to look over the hospital and meet the board members. It's a good opportunity for someone'.

'Yes, thanks again, we'll talk about it'.

I didn't want to leave Scone and Walter. My income was quite enough and I was beginning to get a few shares in some good companies, and moreover I was happy. I couldn't imagine giving up all this.

Yet, as the days went by I began to ask myself whether I wanted to finish up an old man, still a GP in Scone. I had to consider this seriously. Also I realised that as our child and probably children, grew up, schooling would mean many years away at boarding schools. These two questions worried me most. They occupied sufficient of my thoughts to eventually say to RM . . .

'What do you think about this question of going to Adelaide? Have you thought much about it?'

'No, I haven't thought about it. I have no desire to go back to Adelaide to live. I like it here'.

Rosemarie was quite calm and contented. She usually let me make decisions without influencing me. When I said I would like to go and survey the scene in Adelaide, she agreed. So off we went, in the Jaguar with Prue.

We stayed with her parents. Her father was a general practitioner and they were both happy and excited to see us and the baby. RM had a busy time seeing lots of her old friends while I fossicked about the Medical Superintendent scene at the Queen Victoria Maternity Hospital. This was most depressing. The hospital was quite behind the times, needing so much in so many ways. This was understood by the board members who pointed out to me that was precisely why they wanted me. They would make me a member of the board, so that I would have authority to make the necessary changes. I was made to feel welcome by them.

Naturally, this was all very unsettling for me. RM went along quietly in her own dear way.

Eventually in June 1951, I told Walter I was leaving Scone. I remember well, even today, making that dreadful decision. It was so hard for me to tell him. I remember the occasion as we sat together on the couch in my sitting room. I think he may have suspected I was unsettled. I remember his saying . . . 'I should have done the same thing years ago.'

We moved to Adelaide in August 1951.

CHAPTER TWENTY-FOUR

The Last Night

Our last night in Scone was spent with Darvall Kater on his property
'Tarrangower' out on the Bunnan Road. During our last few days, while
packing up was in full swing, he had invited the three of us to stay with
him. We had always been close friends. He had that great affection,
common to older men, for my Rosemarie.

Having been divorced many years ago he had learnt how to manage a
splendid household and his AGA stove. Our last meal of a roast leg of
lamb was preceded with champagne and oysters. His carving of a roast
leg was an exacting surgical procedure, stressing the thickness of each
slice and the removal of the 'gland'. I don't really think this was a gland,
but he always referred to it as such and insisted on its removal, as
though it were something sinister. I think it was just a strip of fat
between two muscle bundles. Anyway after the dissection and the
addition of roast potatoes, peas and cauliflower, all doused with mint
sauce, we began and enjoyed a memorable meal.

Prue had been cotted down earlier. After the basic essentials of tidiness
we relaxed with our brandy and reminisced. We all felt a sadness, for
tomorrow we would part.

Darvall reminded me of the time when he saw two chaps, full of beer,
having a ding-dong fight just outside his gateway, when he came home
one night. Some woman was involved—as usual—and one chap speared
the other in the leg with a hay fork. I had become involved with the
wounds and had to testify to the visiting Stipendiary Magistrate that
these wounds could have been caused in the way Sergeant Bedingfield
had postulated. I hated court appearances. Maybe it was the splendid
meal and the brandy, but I was really quite vague about this whole
episode. It had been some time ago.

'Don't you remember going to court to give evidence? I certainly do,
because this chap was convicted of the assault and taken to Newcastle.
Two nights later our beloved Cocker Spaniel got a strychnine bait and
died a nasty death. I was sure it was someone connected with this chap;
if not it was a mighty strange coincidence,' explained RM.

'Ah yes, I remember it now. It was just a few days before Prue was
born and you cried so much. Our next Cocker never really took his place,
did he?'

'What about that other drunk, in our rose garden. You were away working in hospital in Sydney at the time, but you must remember my telling you about it'.

RM, after a few short years of marriage to me, was beginning to realise that sometimes when she told me a story, she knew it was going in one ear and straight out the other, leaving no mark on my otherwise engaged thoughts.

'Yes, yes, I remember something about it. You told me on the phone; wasn't Lyd Abbott in the story somewhere?'

Lyd was a seventy-year-old spinster who was always terribly frightened—about everything. She lived on her own with all the windows and doors tightly locked.

'Yes, you were away and Lyd had come around to have dinner with me. We were sitting in the drawing room talking after dinner when we heard the strangest noises out in the front garden. I went outside and there in the rose garden was a drunk with one leg up a rose bush, a flagon of wine spilling about, singing away quite happily. Lyd said 'what is it, what is it'? So I told her there was nothing to worry about. It was only a happy drunk who had lost his way and got into our rose garden. I said I would ring up Sergeant Bedingfield. It was Constable Dick who answered the phone. When I told him I had a drunk in the front garden, he said—'have you now'—we both laughed. He said he'd come around. Lyd was so upset—'I'll never get home safely now'. You remember she only lived around the corner from us. Well, anyway, Constable Dick and I got caught on several thorns as we got our happy friend out and dragged him through the gate to the car. Lyd was almost hysterical as she watched, so Constable Dick assured her he would come back and see her safely home. While we waited she was able to steady up enough to enjoy her favourite sweet sherry—dear old Lyd—she was very good to me when you were away, and before I had my own sewing machine. She let me use hers to make a lot of Prue's clothes'.

'Poor old Lyd. She always reminded me of Edna May Oliver; she had that same long face and even that expression. She must have led a lonely life. I always remember the dramas when she had to come to the surgery to see Walter. A full half hour, at least, had to be reserved for these important occasions. The town taxi would bring her and wait for her, with her best hat, her gloves and her handbag. She was quite a character'.

Darvall had known her for a long time. He thought it was a great pity she had never learnt to play bridge. We concluded this talk of Lyd by agreeing that she had been brought up in the Victorian era, when cards for ladies were taboo.

After a pause he asked Rosemarie what she remembered as the funniest thing during her days in Scone.

'Gosh, there've been so many. Les did some funny things, although he rarely meant to. I remember one night when he got to bed fairly late. He was so tired after a week when Walter had been away. He zonked out as soon as he hit the cot. I went on reading quite peacefullly, when the phone rang. He woke, most reluctantly, and growled as he sleepily stretched out his hand and said—'hullo'. He seemed to get no answer and said—'hullo'—again, as I watched the comedy. There he was, lying on his side, eyes closed, saying over and over—'hullo, who's there' until I could contain myself no longer and said—'wake up you ass' put down the light and answer the phone'—just as the exchange gave another ring. I still think that was funny'.

'Yes, well you don't really know how tired and exhausted a busy practice can make you'.

'Oh, I've got a fair idea now. After all, I watched my father struggle for years with one, and now you, so I think I can understand. Just like my mother did. I can remember her telling me a story about Dad. He was having a bad run, full days, with babies at nights for good measure, when he was sound asleep one night as the phone rang. This was just another call so Dad got up and was dressing when Mum said to him—'why don't you let me go dear, I'm sure I could cope?'—'no, no, don't be ridiculous. I have to go. This chap's got his arm stuck up above his head again'.

When he came back he told Mum about his patient, who had a very loose shoulder joint which had been dislocated so often that his wife should have known how to get it into place again—'there you are', she said in her most dramatic manner, 'I could have fixed him'. 'Yes, and what would you have done Joyce?' 'I'd have tickled him under his arm', said mother'.

'Well, she may have been quite right. I must remember that trick'.

Then, after a thoughtful pause I went on—'although in my new life to come, as a specialist obstetrician and gynaecologist, I don't think tickling anywhere would be proper'.

'Certainly not', put in Rosemarie.

Darvall went on to tell the story about a nearby, well respected oldish couple. He was in his mid-sixties, still very upright, grey on top with a military moustache. She, also upright, with a prominent bosom was rather stern in appearance and manner. He told us that when he first came to live in Scone the town gossip suggested some infidelity in this particular camp. It was rumoured that the husband had been impressed by the wife of a nearby neighbour, which impression was apparently mutual. Each had found life boring and rather 'hum-drum' and had searched for new fields for excitement. It was generally believed that they had been successful. Darvall's story went on to relate how, in one particular field, with a high standing crop, a little adultery was proceeding, when a tractor was heard approaching. As it went around the paddock getting nearer and nearer with each circuit the adulterous proceedings ceased, clothing was adjusted and they made to appear, rather weakly, as though they were just out walking. The tractor husband, finding his wife unexpectedly with wheat stalks in her hair, quickly came to the correct conclusion, jumped off the tractor, grabbed his snake-killing wire and gave chase to the military-like gentleman. Being unsuccessful in his pursuit, he gave up his work for the day, refused to talk to his wife, dressed and proceeded to his neighbour's home.

There he found the stern and full bosomed wife who didn't know where her husband was. She thought he had been in town all day.

The cuckold and aggrieved husband spent little time in coming to the point of his visit. The confrontation in the field was explained but to his great surprise the stern mannered and full bosomed wife did not share his emotion. He expected a spirited response.

'This is not the first time I've heard of my husband's involvements. You know, I believe it's a sort of sickness he has!!'

He would wait for another day to discuss this 'sort of a sickness'.

'Do you think that's a true story Darvall?'

'My dear Rosemarie, when you're my age you'll believe anything about the human race, especially it it makes you laugh. I think it's a great country story. If the tractor had only been towing an old fashioned header the consequences could have been horrendous'.

'I won't forget that night at dinner at your place when Mabs and I were there for a game of bridge afterwards. It was your face I remember so well, as your maid at that time, Emily, I think it was, brought the soup in and placed it on the sideboard. She was obviously going out on the town for she came up from the kitchen in short pants, a thin blouse, her hair in pins with a scarf over it and bare feet. You just sat there with your mouth open, trying so hard not to burst out laughing'.

'No, I won't forget it either. Some memories will stay forever. She was quite a girl. On another night we had been out to the Robertsons' and got home near midnight to find Emily and our baby gone. 'Oh, my God,' I said, 'whatever has happened? Where are they?'

'I remember Les rang the police, who came around quickly, arriving at the same time as Emily with Prue, asleep in the pram. She wanted company so had gone off with Prue down town to the Niagara cafe—the meeting place for boys and girls. She'd hoped to get home before us. Les was so furious with her, while I was just happy to know Prue was all right. Her defence was that she had done no wrong as she was still minding Prue!!'

'Her boyfriend, of doubtful habits, turned up with presents for her one night; a new dress and a new pair of shoes. Emily, we presumed, had earned these. The shoes squeaked until they nearly drove RM mad, so she complained. Emily said she'd fix them. She soaked them in water overnight, which stopped the squeaking as both soles had come off. She went on and married this boyfriend but had to wait for six months until his release from Newcastle gaol. The baby came a week before the wedding'.

Another housemaid we had was long in the body, short in the legs and the other end too. She had phenomenal BO which RM tried to correct by making copious gifts of soaps, scents and the best deodorisers of the day. Nothing worked, so she did not stay long. The other one I remember, a tall fair girl, with attractive eyes, was always sighing. She would discuss this with RM who always spent considerable time in the kitchen with her maids. She taught them all how to cook and to keep house. This lass agreed she would have to break this habit of sighing for she had been told that with each sigh she lost a drop of blood!!! People are funny.

'We are going to miss so many things and so much fun here. I wish now I'd not embarked on this move to a new life. Sep thinks I'm mad too, but then we're all a bit mad'.

Rosemarie reminded me—'There was once before when Sep thought you were a bit mad'.

'What, only once?'

'The time I was remembering was when we were driving Betty and Sep back from Sydney in the Buick. It was on dusk when we were nearing Scone. The Aberdeen chooks—don't you remember? There were quite a few on the road, on the little rise just as the road enters Aberdeen. You were doing about fifty and the chooks got nearer, when you said to Sep, sitting in front with you, 'never any need to slow down for chooks, they're more sensible than sheep, they always get out of the way'. The chooks got nearer and nearer until a cloud of white feathers came up in front as you collected a dozen or so. Don't you remember that?'

'Yes, the stupid things, they let me down that day. There was another chook occasion I remember, in the strawberry garden at the back door. The wretched birds were always getting at my berries, so much that I got Harry to put a wire-netting fence around them. I'd come home for lunch and parked at the back door when I saw one large white chook had got in, in spite of the fence. I had an armful of mail including a batch of journals. I grabbed one, took a wild shot which happend to hit it fair in the head. I think I got the greater surprise for the chook didn't live to appreciate the shot. I was also surprised when I carried it in to my next door neighbour with apologies. He abused me. He wasn't a patient of mine, so that may have been the reason.

Darvall thought it was time we all went to bed just as RM began to laugh.

'What do you remember now?' asked Darvall, sitting back again.

'Do you remember after the second day of the Muswellbrook Picnic Races a couple of years ago. We got home about three in the morning and decided we needed more champagne. You should remember, because you were there, when Vic Hall thought we should all have fried eggs on toast. None of you could even get the eggs to fall into the pan when you cracked them. They spilt all over my lovely AGA and down the back of it. I, the girl who is never affected by champagne, had to send you all out of the kitchen. What a mess!'

'I think you are making the whole thing up. I don't remember it'.

'That's only because you tend to forget everything if it's not to do with your work. Maybe tomorrow you won't even remember tonight'.

'Talking of drunks, there was that hilarious night when Sep and Betty came around after dinner with two bottles of special cider he had been given by a grateful client. He said he would teach us 'Cardinal Puff'. This was a silly sort of game, do you know it Darvall?'

'Never heard of it. Tell me'.

'It's a table tapping game with sequences and whenever you make a mistake you must have a drink and start all over again. Les and I were slow to learn. We made many mistakes and so we had to follow the rules, have a drink and start again. I got worse and worse while Betty and Sep did well, they had played before. Les's speech started slipping as well as his vision, so he searched for his glasses to read the label on the bottle. No wonder we were 'squiffy'. He read—'Special Vintage Tasmanian Cider—85 per cent proof'. I really think that is the only time I have been nearly drunk'.

'Vic had a good story about a rabbiter he employed in the mid-thirties. Rabbits were an awful plague on ''Nandowra'' at that time and rabbiters were frequently employed. This particular chap had his wife with him and they set up camp in a far paddock. She became ill and Vic brought her in to see Walter who admitted her to hospital with lobar pneumonia. She became very sick but eventually recovered'.

'Walter had not seen her husband until she was convalescing, a bit strange he thought, but when he did see him he said he had good news for him. His wife would recover and eventually be well again'.

'Oh, I didn't come in about her Doc. It's about meself. I got this awful burning with me water'.

'He had a roaring dose of gonorrhoea. He also had his wife's best friend out in his camp who came up to look after him when she heard about his wife's sickness. She also came up with a message from her husband that he could 'have the use of her' while his wife was sick!!'

'A good story to finish on. We really must go to bed', insisted Darvall.

After we moved to Adelaide we saw very little of Darvall. The last occasion I remember well. We had been in Hawthorn for a few years when one Sunday morning I heard a voice at the back door, 'She must be home, for there are her shoes in the middle of the kitchen floor', as Darvall came in, quite unannounced. He always insisted he saw RM with her shoes more often on the floor than on her feet.

We never saw him again.

POSTSCRIPT

The era of these stories represents, to me, one of civilised medical practice. I believe it represents the end of it.

My introduction to specialised practice transferred me from the peace and happiness of country general practice into a parochial community where I found unexpected and unusual behaviour, riddled with jealousies and their associated intrigues. I regretted my decision.

I eventually learnt to survive and to attain my own security.

The recounting of these next thirty years, watching the rapid decline of the medical profession in Australia, with the associated 'medical fraud' resulting from the introduction of 'Medibank', will challenge me.

L.O.S.P.